Simple Money

Habits and Rules for Saving and Investing that Build Wealth for Everybody

[Second Edition]

Joe Pimbley

Laurel McDevitt

Cover Photo "Bee and Lilac in the flower garden of Virginia McDevitt"

ISBN: 0615864627
ISBN-13: 978-0615864624

Table of Contents

1

INTRODUCTION

Many years ago we read a "financial advice" book that taught that saving and investing now would give future freedom. This freedom was the release from the financial necessity to work. As the author noted, you might certainly choose to continue working, but you would have the freedom to choose. This obvious but powerful idea has remained with us ever since.

We don't remember the names of the book or the author. In fact, it's surprising how little we do remember. The author was a Canadian physician. He wrote at length about the disastrous impact of high inflation on bond investments. That means he likely published the book in the late 1970's. We recall we disagreed with – or more likely did not understand – a few of the investment points he made.

What really matters to us is that one message. Develop good habits now with your personal financial management and you will enjoy future freedom. With this book we send this message of self-earned freedom to a new audience in the hope and expectation that it will help others as the earlier author helped us.

We gain freedom by building wealth. Everybody can build wealth. At a high level, building wealth requires only that we spend less than we earn and invest the difference. Subsequent chapters fill in the details, but it's ultimately this simple. Money is simple.

Freedom is enabling and ennobling. With financial security, you have the option to be charitable with family, friends, and society. Your charitable contributions can consist of your time devoted to worthy projects since you are able to work without monetary compensation. Time is more valuable than money, yet money can buy time.

Exit
Financial
Freedom
Years Ahead
30

2

Money is Simple

Money is simple. Money is good. Why do we resist so strenuously these self-evident truths?

Free Market Exchange

Let's start at the beginning. Every adult must acquire the survival necessities of food, shelter, and clothing. The most direct means of acquisition is to grow one's own food, build one's own shelter, and make one's own clothing. Free people, however, choose otherwise. Just as baking two pies is little more effort than baking one, production of food, shelter, and clothing admits vast economies of scale. A farmer can double the size of his "garden" to feed two families rather than one without doubling his labor or investment in tools. By doubling his production, the farmer will exchange the excess crops, perhaps, for the clothing and firewood that his neighbor provides.

The superior efficiency of this exchange, or "barter", system is indisputable. All participants in this barter system earn their necessities with less time and effort. The heightened efficiency increases survival probability in "lean years" and, in good times, enables pursuit of happiness in the form of, for example, recreation and entertainment. Voluntary participation is the ingenious element that powers gains in productivity through barter. A central authority that mandates exchange of a farmer's excess crops will find a mysterious inability of the farmer to produce the excess. Forcible coercion of the farmer is tyranny that generates want and starvation. Economic and political orders are inseparable.

Exchange of construction nails for grains

Money Solves the Exchange Rate Problem

Direct barter is manageable in small communities but suffers from the complexity of innumerable "exchange rates" among the barter items (*e.g.*, vegetables, meat, clothing, livestock, lumber, barn construction, medical services, *et cetera*). The establishment of "money" simplifies the barter system tremendously. People exchange their goods and services for money that they use, in turn, to exchange for items they need from others. Money becomes the pre-eminent barter item but has meaning only in its ability to facilitate free market exchange of goods and services.

Money is an extraordinarily simple and elegant solution to the barter exchange rate problem. Further, the size and scope of the barter market increases astronomically due to our ability to save money for future years, borrow money for future repayment, and transmit money easily over long distances. All human societies invent money, just as they discover fire, in their pursuit of survival and advancement.

So, money is both simple and necessary for a prosperous community. Money is also clearly "good" since its mere existence expands and promotes the barter that brings elevated productivity that, in turn, leads to enhanced survival and pursuit of happiness.

Barter Continues Today

Though we've used language and examples thus far that denote earlier times when survival was more challenging, professions limited, and luxuries few, the same concepts apply today. Free markets still depend on the barter system in which money is the primary barter item. Money remains simple, ingenious, and good. Most people receive money in exchange for their services as employees of corporate or government entities. With this money they purchase necessities of food, shelter, and clothing as well as healthcare and luxuries. Money left unspent is "savings" and different people choose to save different amounts of money for themselves.

Just as the existence of money is "good" for the prosperity of the entire community, money that an individual retains in savings is also "good" both for the individual and the community. First and foremost, savings are insurance against loss of income. It's always possible that a person's income will fall dramatically due, for example, to loss of employment. Such loss of income with insufficient savings may drain taxpayers' savings if the government subsidizes the indigent citizen. The protection a person's savings account provides against unemployment is even more beneficial to the person himself than to the community as a whole. Loss of income is an ever-present threat that produces anxiety and stress. The level of anxiety and stress, however, is much less when there exists enough savings to withstand a prolonged income loss. Money in savings, therefore, reduces stress and thereby improves quality of life.

It's not difficult to find numerous other reasons why saving money is good. Savings permit you to pay for your own retirement without burdening family and government (*i.e.*, your fellow citizens). Available money gives you choices you wouldn't otherwise have in terms of healthcare, education, adoption, housing, or any other quality of life aspect. Savings also give you the means to help others through charity. As the old saying relates, "to do good, you must first do well". People who choose not to save money cannot be charitable with money.

In the early 1980's we read a book on investment advice. As we described earlier, the author was a Canadian physician. We have only one clear memory of his counsel. This author forcefully argued that financial independence gives true freedom. When we save and invest, we will eventually reach the time (before retirement) when we need not work. We may still choose to work, but financial straits do not force us to do so. This is true freedom, the freedom to walk away from employment.

Hostility to the Rich?

And yet, there's something wrong here. Our society

harbors ambivalence, and sometimes hostility, for "the rich". This phrase has an undeniable negative connotation, but why? Rich people are simply those who have saved much of their income, or have invested well, or have received money from others. Rich people, generally speaking, donate more to charities than others and do not claim benefits from taxpayers.

The classic media characterization of "the rich" is Charles Dickens' Ebenezer Scrooge. What a stereotype! Scrooge is old, bitter, abusive, miserly, and cheerless. He's a detriment to society. The tale implies Scrooge is wealthy because he abuses others, is stingy, and pores over his pitiless accounts for long hours every day.

Ebenezer Scrooge is fiction. But he reflects and infects some subconscious attitudes we all have of the rich. Clearly, society should censure any person who lies, cheats, or steals to gain money (or anything else). The great majority of rich people do not lie, cheat, or steal to gain their wealth. They simply earn more than they spend and invest the difference. Dickens' *The Christmas Carol* is great entertainment and teaches a valuable lesson. But it also plants some faulty wiring in our brains that may sabotage our money management. Thrift is a virtue. Financial success comes from hard work and good decisions. We'll believe the Scrooge stereotype is waning when parents start to name their sons "Ebenezer" again!

Here's a non-fictional anecdote of hostility to the rich. In recent years an English couple won a substantial sum in a lottery of some sort in Britain. This couple pondered and chose not to move their family. They decided not to buy a newer, bigger, more luxurious house. This decision angered the neighbors. One woman told the newly wealthy couple (paraphrase): "If you don't move, we will. We can't stand to live near people with so much money." Call it an "Alec Baldwin moment".

The label that fits this behavior is "class envy" which is more prevalent in Europe than in the US. Finding a label, though, does not explain the hostility. Society openly approves of ordinary people <u>seeking</u> wealth in the venues of television game shows or lotteries but then ostracizes those who succeed. It makes no sense. For reasons unknown, we develop complicated, contradictory, and often secretive views of money and its meaning in childhood. Yet, as we've argued, money is simple. There's very little of substance over which rational people would disagree.

Wealth is not "Quality"

Why does society vilify wealth? Perhaps the emotional tension surrounding money derives from a connection between wealth, which is easy to measure, and the inherent value of a person. If so, let's state the obvious: a person's wealth does <u>not</u> measure his/her "quality". A wealthy person is merely good at making and managing money or lucky enough to have received money. That's it. Otherwise, this person can be just as rude, inconsiderate, unpleasant, and opinionated as anybody else.

Wealth does not measure "quality". The ultimate "quality person" in living memory is, most likely, Mother Teresa whose "wealth measurement" was a nice, round number ("zero"). We should all aspire to good works for family and community and pursuit of happiness. Managing our money well can help us in both aspects but wealth is <u>not</u> the measurement of how we fulfill these aspirations.

So, gaining wealth will not make you a better person. Wealth won't even solve most of your problems. Perhaps only rich people can truly understand the adage "money doesn't buy happiness". Still, for reasons of lower stress and the ability to support oneself and help others, we should all choose to build wealth. We need to abandon the Scrooge stereotype of wealth! Money is good.

3

RICH HABITS

Everybody should be rich. Anybody *can* be rich. Are these ridiculous statements? Try to find the flaw in the logic of this chapter!

First, let's waffle just a little bit. To gain wealth, we must first be able to earn income or find money somewhere. If a person is chronically unemployed and simply cannot or will not find and hold a job, then true financial wealth is unattainable. We apply the "anybody can be rich" statement, then, only to people with ability to earn income (almost all of us).

Definition of "Rich"

More importantly, we must define "rich" and "wealthy". Any definition will be somewhat arbitrary. It's tempting to choose "millionaire" – a person with net worth of $1 million or more – for this wealth threshold. But this net worth value is popular only because it's such a "round number". We prefer instead to define "wealthy" and "rich" as a person who has savings and investments equal to or greater than ten times his/her annual, pre-tax income. For example, if your annual income is $50,000, you're rich if you have $500,000 or more in the bank. Your wealth, then, is relative to your earning power.

It would certainly be a mistake to define "wealthy" as something like "people with income (or assets) in the top 1% of all Americans". This definition makes 1% of the population wealthy by construction. It forces a negative view of wealth in that you must "beat out" others to be wealthy. Life and wealth are not a competition! Everybody can win! The purpose of wealth is not to "be better" or "feel better" than others. Money can't do that for you. Rather, as the last chapter discussed, wealth improves the quality of your life by reducing anxiety (dependence on current income) and enabling you to provide for your own retirement. Defining your wealth, then, as holding ten times your current income in savings and investments is far more rational than creating a "money game" in which you must have more than others.

Simple Strategy

The wealth strategy is stunningly simple. It's so simple that everybody already "knows" it. They merely choose not to execute it! To paraphrase Benjamin Franklin, "income of 20 pence and expenses of 19 pence make a wealthy man." That's all. Just spend less than you make and invest the difference.

Here's how it works. Your current annual income may be $20,000, $50,000, $100,000 or whatever. If you save and invest 10% of this income year after year, it will grow to ten times your income in 24 years. We've taken the average investment rate to be 10% per year, which is typical of large capitalization stocks over a long time horizon. This 24-year period may seem quite long … and that's true. But after those 24 years you'll be much happier to have saved and invested than you will if you've chosen not to save. (Would you prefer to be 24 years older and wealthy or just 24 years older?) Further, this 24-year period falls to 18 years if you save 20%, rather than 10%, of each paycheck.

This analysis ignores inflation since inflation will not change the results if both your income and the average investment rate increase similarly. But it's also reasonable to consider your income may grow faster than inflation as your workplace value increases. Increasing income is good! When your income grows 3% per year faster than inflation, the time period for acquiring ten times your original income with 10% savings rate falls to 22 years while the period for gaining ten times the current income grows to 30 years.

We've also skated over the annoying but relevant tax issue. The analysis assumes you save and invest 10% of your pre-tax income while the average investment rate – also 10% - is an after-tax return. The pre-tax return that gives you 10% after you pay taxes depends on your specific tax rate. A reasonable estimate is that you'll need to earn 12% pre-tax in order to realize 10% after taxes.

Again, this is clearly not the "fast track" to wealth, but it works! It's also quite painless in that you need put aside only 10-20% of your income. There's no reason, of course, to restrict yourself to this level of savings. Consider 10% of income as the minimum.

How the Strategy Fails

If the wealth strategy is so simple, why is everybody not wealthy or on the path to wealth? There are two primary reasons. First, many people do not invest wisely. Remaining chapters of this book discuss investments in detail. As a quick preview, all of us must define our risk tolerance and buy only acceptable investments that fit this tolerance. Investing is much simpler than it appears.

The greatest reason for the failure of the strategy is failure to execute! Most of us simply choose not to save. We use the word "choose" to emphasize that we do control our own spending. Rich people are not rich because they are "lucky" to have high income. Many high-income people, in fact, are not wealthy because they spend what they earn. Conversely, many rich people do not have high incomes. They simply know how to save, invest, and manage their money.

It may be that there exists a person somewhere in the country who absolutely cannot survive on 90% of current income and must have the full 100%. For all other non-savers, though, the fundamental problem is the choice to incur many unnecessary expenses. For example, a person or family accustomed to annual income of $40,000 can almost certainly live well on $35,000.*

The Debt Trap

Imagine you want to save money and claim it's not possible. The bills arrive in the mail every month and sweep away all the after-tax income. Is that possible? Sure! Many of the bills are principal and interest for home mortgages, home equity loans, car loans, and credit card payments. You've got to pay them. The choice to borrow and incur debt was the "choice" not to save and invest.

Though loans can be helpful, they are also dangerous. Avoid them. Borrow only for your house since houses are both expensive relative to income and necessary. There's no need,

* Notice that we set this income level at $35,000 rather than $36,000 (90% of $40,000). This is an approximate correction for the impact of income taxes. Earning $40,000 and pushing 10% ($4,000) into savings may leave the person or family with roughly the same remaining after-tax income as earning $35,000 and saving nothing.

however, to buy the most expensive house a bank will permit you to finance. Buy what you need and like. When it comes to cars, furniture, appliances, home remodeling and everything else, pay cash. If you can't pay cash, your attitude should be that you cannot afford the purchase. It's fine to take the cash from your investments. This discipline forces you to save the money first and then buy what you want. You'll see clearly the "cost" of your new furniture if you see the deduction from your savings rather than a new monthly payment.

This advice may seem overly conservative and paternalistic. After all, if we can take out a loan to buy the car we want now rather than waiting two years to save the money, we'll have the car two years early! Everybody wins. A smart financial person can argue correctly that the car loan makes sense even when we're able to pay cash. The loan allows us to keep the cash invested at, hopefully, a return greater than the loan interest rate. (See our discussion of investment "leverage" in "Acceptable Investments" in chapter 6.)

The bigger problem is the psychology of the loan. Many people use the freedom that borrowing provides to trap themselves. The debt service (principal and interest) payments deplete their ability to save. The best solution is avoidance of all forms of debt to the greatest extent possible.

For example, credit cards furnish extraordinary convenience. You don't need cash in your wallet or purse to pay for goods and services. With the credit card, you get a bill a few weeks later. In fact, it saves you money since you earn interest in your checking account for those weeks. If you don't pay that bill immediately, though, then you're really borrowing money with the credit card. This is the worst debt of all since the interest rates are as high as 20% and the borrowing itself is insidious. Every credit card purchase you make becomes a new loan.

Appearance of Wealth

Since money is "good" and since attaining wealth is "simple" (spend less than you make and invest the difference), why do so few of us build our wealth? Our discussion thus far points to our choice <u>not</u> to save a small portion of our income. The monthly bills of the "debt trap" suck away all our income. Why do we incur the debt? The reasons may go beyond carelessness to a fundamental, though subconscious, misunderstanding of wealth and money management.

We argue that wealth is the accumulation of savings most of which is in the form of investments (stocks, bonds, and mutual funds). Wealthy people have savings of this sort equal to or greater than ten times their current income. True wealth improves quality of life by reducing stress and anxiety and gives people a large measure of financial freedom. The wealthy may, or may not, choose to buy a more impressive house than they need, a nicer car, or more expensive furniture.

Many of us miss the in-between step of owning substantial investments and go straight to the consumption of owning the impressive house, nice car, and expensive furniture. That is, we mistakenly believe that we measure wealth by the grandeur of our houses, cars, and furniture. These are the wrong measurements. When we spend as much as we can in the present on luxurious items, we rob our future wealth by choosing not to save and invest.

Just as measuring wealth with the opulence of our houses, cars, and furniture is misguided, so too is our notion of what we can "afford". Quite often, if our bank, car dealer, or furniture salesperson will lend us the money to pay for our purchase, then we consider the transaction to be prudent. The lender simply reviews our income and other expenses and judges whether we can squeeze in this new monthly bill payment. Piling up expenses against our income drives our view of what we can "afford".

But these expenses prevent us from saving money regularly to build wealth. This attitude, then, that we can afford purchases whenever we find a willing lender destroys our future wealth. We should borrow money only for purchasing houses. For everything else, if we cannot pay cash (from savings), then we cannot "afford" whatever it is we want.

Turn It Around

If you've not been saving a portion of your income and recognize yourself in this discussion, then turn it around. It's never too late (unless, as Yogi Berra might say, it's too late). Here are four suggestions. First, stop borrowing. If you cannot pay your entire credit card balance, for example, then stop using all credit cards now. Each credit card purchase is a loan. No more loans! Take out the scissors and cut up those cards if that's what it takes to stop using them.

Second, ruthlessly pare back your monthly expenses. You must pay the electricity bill, but you can increase vigilance to avoid wasting electricity. Ask yourself if you really need movie channels on the television. (We say you don't!) Review your telephone bills to determine if your "plan" charges you for features you do not use or need. Instead of buying books, borrow them whenever possible from your local library. We hope the book you're holding now is a library book!

Third, deliberately "pay" your savings account every week or month the amount of money you wish to save (at least 10% of pre-tax income). That is, let the savings be your first expense. The idea is that this action will force you to reduce discretionary expenses (*e.g.*, meals out and other unnecessary purchases) if such expenses have been making saving impossible.

Finally, adopt the attitude that your expenses need not rise if your income rises. Specifically, if your income rises, that's good! Consider this event an opportunity to increase your savings rate. Don't automatically increase your expenses to match the increased income. The suggestion is obvious, but we do tend to believe we "deserve more" if our income increases. Forget the "deserve more" temperament and change it to "save more".

4

MOVING YOUR MONEY

Though a basic point, let's be clear about where your money sits. All of us pay for items daily with cash in our pockets, checks, credit cards, or on-line banking services. The bank checking account is the "central storage place" for these immediate cash needs. When we need real cash, we visit one of our bank's automated teller machines (ATMs) to make a withdrawal from the checking account. We write checks to pay weekly and monthly bills (or pay such bills on-line). The checking account eventually pays for credit card purchases when we pay the credit card bill itself.

Checking accounts, then, are necessary and useful. They also pay little or no interest and, therefore, are not investments. Holding money in the checking account is not investing. You must determine a "safe level" of cash to hold in the checking account (generally 2-4 weeks of typical expenses). Ideally, you will deposit a steady income, such as salary, into the checking account so that the income exceeds the expenses. (If expenses usually outpace income, that's a big problem! See "Rich Habits" in chapter 3.) When this account balance grows beyond your safe level, you'll send the excess money to your "investment account".

The Investment Account

The investment account is not a "savings account" and is not a bank CD (certificate of deposit), an investment we discuss later. Rather, your investment account is a separate account you open with a "broker" (such as *TD Ameritrade*, *Morgan Stanley*, *Fidelity Investments*, *et cetera*). Some larger banks (*e.g.*, *Citigroup*, *JPMorgan Chase*) will also offer brokerage accounts to their banking clients. The key aspect of these brokerage (or investment) accounts is that you send your money and then tell the broker which investments to buy on your behalf.

You choose a broker as you would choose a bank or any other service provider. (See also chapter 12 on "Financial Advisors".) You consider convenience of access, recommendations of friends, and public reputation. Since you're sending money, it's critically important to ask how you and your money are protected against fraud and bankruptcy of the broker. In almost all cases you'll learn that the US government insures your account with the Securities Investor Protection Corporation ("SIPC", see the web site *http://www.sec.gov/answers/sipc.htm*). This insurance protects your securities in the brokerage account (up to $500,000) if the broker declares bankruptcy or becomes insolvent for any reason.* That's an excellent guarantee. Be sure you have this protection. Still, never – ever - send your money to a firm that sounds unfamiliar to you (even with the SIPC insurance).

Let's be clear about this $500,000 insurance. This insurance does **not** protect you from losses in your investments. The protection only pertains to the risk that the bank or broker to which you've trusted your money enters bankruptcy. If you send $40,000 to the broker to purchase *Google* stock and the value of this stock later falls to half its earlier value, you lose $20,000. There's no insurance against this "market loss".

With brokers, though, there's another level of choice: full-service or discount. Full-service brokers charge higher fees and stand ready to give much advice and recommendations. They will meet with you to discuss your finances, teach you what you want and need to know, and give you more written information and ideas than you can ever possibly read. If such a broker does his/her job well and if you develop a good relationship with him/her **and** if you feel the teaching and advice benefits you,

* Ordinary bank accounts have $250,000 "FDIC insurance" to protect you from the bank's insolvency.

then the broker deserves the higher fees. If you don't get along well with the broker, then find another. This is important! If you don't trust or respect your broker or if you don't receive the trust and respect you deserve, then try again with somebody else. If you're unsure as to whether you should try the full-service or discount broker, choose full-service. You can always switch later when you become more expert.

Discount brokers, by contrast, often charge amazingly low fees. For example, a typical on-line discount broker may charge fees only for buying and selling stocks and bonds and the typical fee is $20 or less. That is, if you buy $20,000 of stock, this broker would charge $20. The full-service broker may charge $400 for the same trade. It's a huge difference. This discount broker, though, will likely give no advice whatsoever. The only service may be a monthly report of your investments (very important, of course). They'll give you no market research and you'll never meet a real person. You're on your own!

There are also firms in between these two extremes of high-cost/high-service and low-cost/low-service. Some discount brokers will provide much research for clients on their web site. Some full-service brokers will cut fees by providing a broker with whom you interact only by telephone.

It can't hurt to start with the full-service broker and decide to switch, or not to switch, in the following years. Our later discussion of "risk tolerance" and investment choices will add more to the proper conduct of full-service brokers.

Opening an Investment Account

Whether in-person or by telephone or Internet, opening an investment account is so straightforward that it hardly warrants much discussion. Walk into the local branch of the bank that holds your checking account business. Instead of heading for the lines at the teller windows, look around and you'll see other cubicles or small offices with "investment representatives" – as they're called. Stand in line for these investment people. They'll sit you down and create an investment account for you and most likely link it to your checking account.

You need not choose the bank that holds your checking business, of course. You can walk into any bank or other physical office of a prominent "asset management firm" of good reputation. See these lists that show nearly 200 such firms in the U.S., Canada, and Europe: http://en.wikipedia.org/wiki/List_of_asset_management_firms .

As we mentioned above, however, always deal with a firm you "know of" or have "heard of". If you see a name on a list or hear a recommendation of an unfamiliar firm, investigate deliberately and with caution before sending money or providing personal information. As an example, let's consider *AllianceBernstein* since it's one of the first names that appears in the linked list. This firm is likely completely unknown to the great majority of people outside the finance industry. But a simple *Google* search of "AllianceBerstein" shows hundreds of thousands of hits. Opening just a few of these links and perusing the *AllianceBernstein* website both show this is a known, legitimate, and substantial asset manager.

There's no need to be restricted to brokerage/investment firms that have physical locations other than the comfort of speaking to employees in person. Search on the Internet for well-known names (*Fidelity*, *TD Ameritrade*, *Putnam*, *Eaton Vance*, *et cetera*) or names from a trusted list. Most of the websites permit you to open accounts on-line. Otherwise or in addition, these sites will provide telephone numbers for opening accounts. Whether by website or telephone or physical meeting, always run your Internet diligence search on any firm you may select as your investment account provider.

Investments in the Investment Account

Largely speaking, your money in the investment account will be in one of two buckets: risk-free, immediately available cash or "risky investments". The first bucket, which we'll call the "money market account" or the "cash account", is like a checking account with a good interest rate. Money you send to your investment account will go directly to this cash account. It's the account for money that you have not yet decided how to invest. You will always keep at least 20% of your total investments in this cash account in case you urgently need money "back home" or to let you act immediately on a good (investment) buying opportunity. The cash in this cash account is not as accessible as that in your real checking account. It may take three business days to receive cash you withdraw. Ideally, you will only take money out of the (investment) cash account for major purchases (house, car, college tuition payments, *et cetera*).

Though it may sound complicated at first, there's not much to know about your broker's money market funds. You want a fund with no commission charges for buying or selling. The government regulations that constrain the activities of money market funds make them extremely safe. It is almost impossible to lose money in such funds, so we call them "risk-free". (Neither will you make much money. This is just a "cash storage account".) For an extra level of security, you should ask the broker if he/she has "triple-**A**" rated money market funds. We explain the meaning of ratings at more length in our discussion of bonds in chapter 9. Alternatively, choose a money market fund that invests only in US government ("Treasury") debt obligations. The risk of loss is essentially zero and investors do not pay state taxes on the interest income of such funds. (In chapter 14, "Tax Considerations", we suggest that investors <u>avoid</u> excessive focus on tax considerations for investments.)

The "risky" investments comprise about 80% of the total investment account. The word "risky" is not equivalent to "bad" or "inappropriate". Rather, "risky" simply means that there is no certainty on the value of the investment for the next day, week, month, or year. Different investors have very different tolerances for risk. The first rule of investing is to take risk that is "comfortable" for you. We devote chapter 5 on "Risk Tolerance" to this topic.

The universe of risky investments is huge. The most popular, that we will discuss at some length in chapters 8 and 9, are corporate stocks and bonds. Since virtually anything you can buy has the potential to appreciate in value, you may consider most assets to be "investments". But let's leave aside the more eccentric possibilities (such as rare coins, fine wine, precious stones, artwork, 70's-era lava lamps) and restrict ourselves to financial investments. Other major investments are real estate, commodities (such as oil, gold, platinum, wheat), partnerships, and currencies. Commodity and currency investments generally take the form of futures contracts and options on futures contracts. Partnerships are business organizations that pool funds to invest in commodities or real estate. See "Exotic, Unacceptable Investments" in chapter 11 for more information on the curious alternatives.

Like partnerships, mutual funds solicit cash from investors so that the fund managers can purchase and manage other investments (usually stocks and bonds). Hedge funds are lightly regulated (and yet restricted) mutual funds.

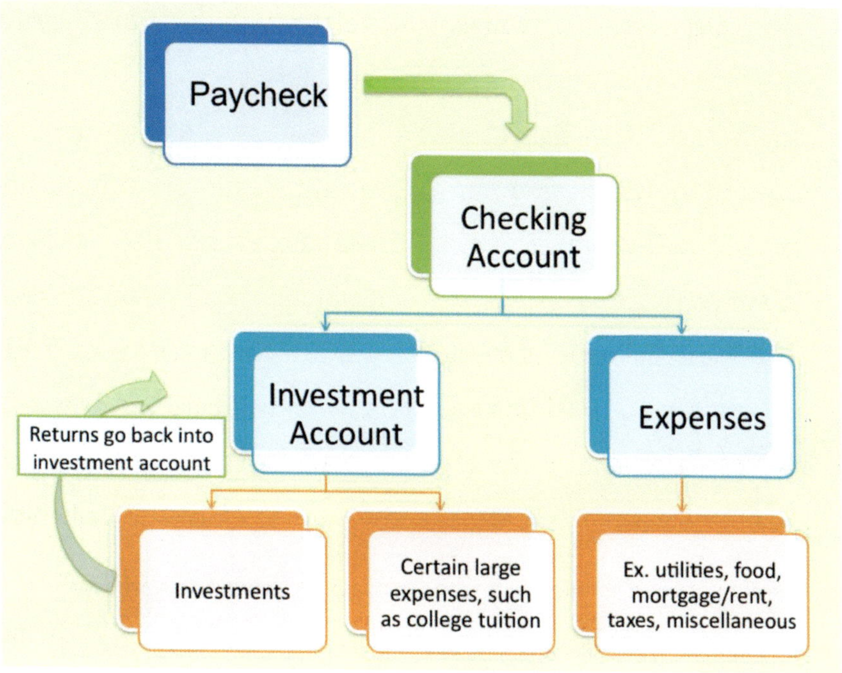

5

RISK TOLERANCE

One of this book's most important lessons is "know what you're buying". Another, more basic, lesson is "know yourself". Two people (or two families) that are financially identical (*i.e.*, similar age, income, present and future expenses) in every way will and should have different investment strategies due to differing attitudes toward risk.

Meaning of Risk

Let's discuss in detail what we mean by "risk". In finance, "risk" is the uncertainty of the outcome of an investment decision. While every investment has an expected outcome, the actual result of a risky investment may be higher or lower than this expectation. So there's "good risk" (gaining more than expected) and "bad risk" (gaining less than expected or even losing). Roughly speaking, both the possible gain and the possible loss increase as the risk of an investment increases. You must expose yourself to risk of loss if you seek the "risk" of gain.

An example of a risk-free investment is a 3-month Treasury bill (debt obligation of the United States government). If you buy this "T-bill" today, you will unquestionably receive your investment back in three months with known interest. There will be no "good surprises" in which you receive more than you expect. Conversely, there will be no "bad surprises". The actual rate of interest you receive in this T-bill is known as the "risk-free rate" for the T-bill's maturity. Bank deposits and certificates of deposit (CDs) that the US government guarantees through the FDIC (Federal Deposit Insurance Corporation) are also risk-free investments. We also consider most money market funds (those that invest only in US government obligations or have a prominent credit rating agency's triple-**A** designation) to be the only remaining risk-free alternatives.

There aren't many risk-free investments. All others are "risky" in the sense that the outcome is uncertain. The risk of different risky investments varies widely from "very low" to "outright gamble". A key element of finance holds that an investment's <u>expected</u> return increases as its risk increases. Though the expected (or average) return of a risky investment may differ from the actual outcome, this expected return is higher for riskier ventures. For example, the expected return of all risky investments is greater than the risk-free rate (the expected and actual return of a risk-free investment).

The extra return you earn in a risky investment is the "risk premium". The market pays the risk premium to investors who are willing to bear the risk of risky investments. When we say "the market pays the risk premium", we mean that the market price of the risky asset is less than it would be if this asset held no risk. The market gives a "discount" for risky investments.

Personalization of Risk

With choices of zero-, low-, or high-risk investments, what's the right strategy? There is none! A supreme consideration for each investor is his/her own tolerance for risk. With a portfolio size of, say, $100,000, you can easily lose or make thousands of dollars each day with moderate-risk stocks. Some people literally lose sleep over this uncertainty. The purpose of saving and investing is to make your life better. Thus, you should not make risky investments if the level of risk disturbs you.

Risk-free or low-risk portfolios will never produce gains of 20% or more per year, but neither will they fall in value. There will be years in which the low-risk choice is best. While it's true, then, that high-risk investments will outperform lower risk alternatives, on average over many years, it is not fair to claim that the former are, therefore, "better". High-risk investors have a greater chance of gaining wealth in a short time than the rest of us. They also have a greater chance of losing it all.

There are two points here. First, you must find your own risk comfort level. Choosing low-risk investments is not at all irrational. Second, there is no "free lunch". Investments with the potential to "win big" also have the potential to "lose big". When you choose fairly risky investments, be sure you understand that the possibility of loss is almost as large as the possibility of gain. Through our own friends and acquaintances, we learned that the surging stock market of the 1990's brought in many first-time investors near the end of the decade. Unfortunately, many put all their money into the riskier NASDAQ stocks and lost as much as 50% of their investments. It's likely the upward trend of the market deceived these people regarding the risk of suffering losses.

Neither is it irrational to be a high-risk investor. If you're comfortable with the prospect that you may lose the entire investment, then high-risk investing can be fun and profitable. You'll win some and lose some. Your enthusiasm for high-risk investing may coax you to save more for the investments which will, in turn, build your wealth faster.

If both low- and high-risk investing are "not irrational", then what is irrational? Fortunately, all investments in efficient markets are fairly priced (see chapter 7 for Efficient Markets). Thus, all such investments are rational as long as you don't use leverage and you can afford a complete loss.

An example of a truly irrational investment is any lottery ticket. If the government regulated lottery tickets as investments, they'd be illegal! Prices of lottery tickets are far greater than "fair value" in terms of expected reward. If you can do without the entertainment value of the lottery, we advise you to save these funds for true investments. You'll be much more likely to gain true wealth.

The financial world also has its own irrational investments. We reviewed a partnership transaction for friends that brokers sold to retail clients (*i.e.*, people like you and me). Amazingly, though the investment held many risks, the pricing gave the investors no risk premium. That is, the brokers were selling to investors at inflated prices. It's certainly irrational to take risk and not receive the proper risk premium. This partnership trade was not liquid and had no price transparency. One moral, then, is to invest only in efficient market securities.

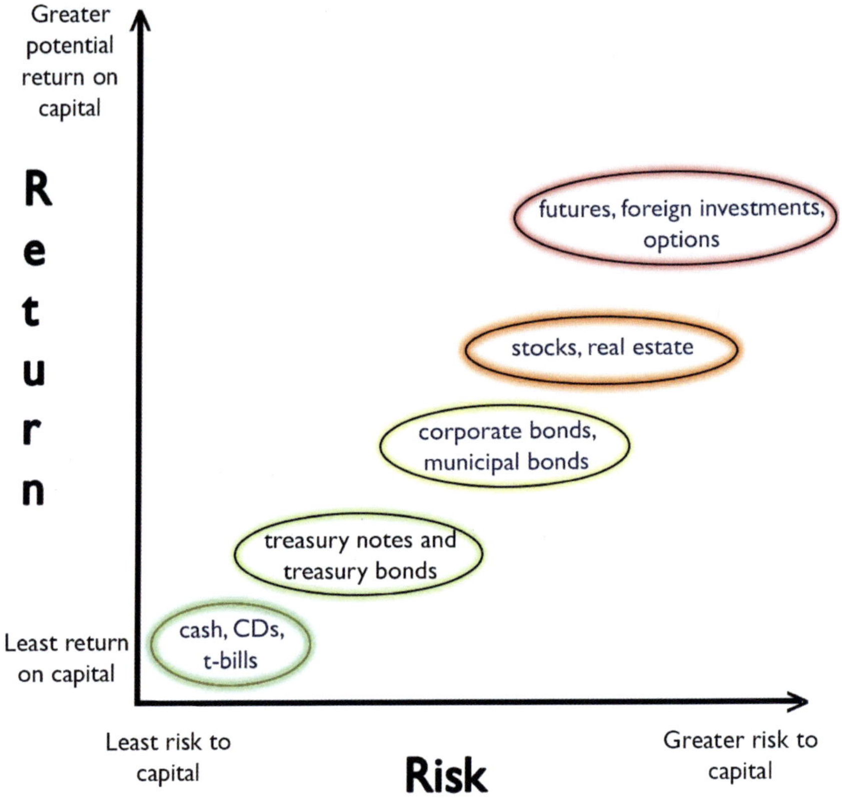
Greater potential return on capital
Return
futures, foreign investments, options
stocks, real estate
corporate bonds, municipal bonds
treasury notes and treasury bonds
Least return on capital
cash, CDs, t-bills
Least risk to capital
Risk
Greater risk to capital

6

PRINCIPLES OF ACCEPTABLE INVESTMENTS

There's no single investment or investment plan that suits all people … even those who appear identical in all financial respects. Chapter 5 on "risk tolerance" discusses this critical topic. Still, there do exist principles that apply to all individual investors. We list the principles here, elaborate on them, and then describe in detail investments that are "acceptable" in view of these principles.

Principles for Individual Investors

First, **stay within your risk tolerance**. If you're not comfortable with the risk of an investment, don't make the investment. Don't let your advisor or friends or anybody tell you how much risk you should take with **your** investment. Your risk tolerance may change over time, but the change must be your decision.

Second, **be prepared to suffer a <u>complete loss</u> on any risky investment**. If the consequences of a complete loss on an investment portfolio (*e.g.*, you can't send children to a private college, you need to postpone retirement, *et cetera*) are completely unbearable for you, then keep your money in risk-free investments: money market funds; bank CDs; and Treasury debt securities (to be discussed). Of course, it's quite extreme to posit that all your risky investments will fall to zero value. This is a "doomsday scenario" that almost certainly will not happen. Still, never make a risky investment that you can't afford to lose.

Third, **know what you're buying**. Don't make any investment you don't understand. All of finance is comprehensible. If you don't understand an investment, then most likely your advisor hasn't explained it well. If you're a highly paid athlete or entertainer, you may be tempted to pay somebody else to "worry about your money". We advise you to worry about your own money. Of course, "worry" is the wrong word. Just manage it. The advisor, if you have one, can make suggestions and recommendations. But you're "the man" (or "the woman") with your own money.

Fourth, **all investments must be liquid**. By "liquid", we mean you should be able to sell them within one business day. (The broker may not be able to send cash back to you for three days even though he/she has sold the asset on the day of your request.) This liquidity requirement is **not** simply for the convenience of permitting you to raise cash quickly. Rather, it encourages you to maintain your investments in "efficient markets". When markets panic, illiquid assets fall fastest in value and, worst of all, you may not be able to sell at any price. With this reasoning, your house is not a suitable investment and neither are your wine collection or Hummel figurines. You're free to buy a house, wine, and collectibles, of course. Just do not consider them as investments.

Fifth, **make only those investments the values of which you can follow on a daily basis**. That is, the investment value should appear daily in the *Wall Street Journal* or other newspapers or publicly accessible sources. If not, then the "price transparency" (another hallmark of efficient markets) of the investment is inadequate.

Sixth, **never borrow money to make investments**. A popular word in finance for borrowing to invest is "leverage". Only professional investors should use leverage (or "lever themselves"). For example, leverage drives the entire banking industry. Banks borrow from depositors and lend to homeowners and businesses. Leverage supercharges a portfolio. You'll make money twice as fast when times are good and lose it twice as fast otherwise. That may sound like a good trade-off to some, but leverage is what drove investors in

1929 to jump out of windows. Even though leverage is arguably safe in the right circumstances, follow the wisdom of many painful experiences and avoid it!

Seventh, and finally, **diversify your investments**. As the old saying goes, don't put all your eggs in one basket. We love old sayings because they usually express deep truths in deceptively simple terms. (The examples of "Time heals all wounds", "Virtue is its own reward", and "Waste not, want not" come to mind.) We speak at more length about diversification in a later chapter.

There are ample events over the years to illustrate each of these principles. Here we quickly discuss one for each of the last four.

Long Term Capital Management (LTCM), the *Titanic* of hedge funds, sank spectacularly in 1998. Though it's a complicated story, it's fair to say the partners were leading experts on capital markets and risk management. They deliberately leveraged themselves to an extraordinary extent and placed themselves in illiquid investment positions. It's not that the partners were stupid (though, in the end, "smart" and "stupid" sometimes become indistinguishable). They'd been taking the same positions for years and making tons of money. When the markets became unusually choppy, the illiquidity of LTCM's positions coupled with the leverage forced the hedge fund to take huge losses. Sober-minded, professional investors can successfully manage illiquid <u>or</u> leveraged investments. The combination of illiquidity and leverage will topple anybody.

In 1994, a professional named David Askin ran a hedge fund specializing in complicated mortgage-backed securities (MBS). Roughly speaking, these MBS were similar to bonds with the exception that it was never clear when the bonds would pay back the principal (the most important feature of a bond!). The fund blew up and lost half a billion dollars because the lenders to the fund (leverage!) disagreed with Askin on the value of the MBS. The MBS did not have "price transparency" and, in fact, nobody really knew what they were worth. Askin himself had created sophisticated mathematical models to argue for his valuations. He may have been right. It doesn't matter. The hedge fund is gone.

There's a pattern here. The two examples thus far as well as the next two all have "leverage" as a key ingredient for disaster. So let's pause and emphasize the lesson. Don't borrow to invest. For example, forget the home equity loan. Close your ears to the siren song of a friend or broker who tells you how much "easier" it will be to make money if you borrow. Leverage is for professionals … and they burn themselves often enough.

The Orange County Investment Pool in 1994 gives a pure leverage story. The manager borrowed billions of dollars to buy long maturity US Treasury debt obligations ("Treasuries" or "Treasury bonds"). These Treasuries have no default risk, are highly liquid, and have unbeatable price transparency. The manager apparently found what he thought was an arbitrage, a way to make money with no risk as we discuss in chapter 7. He borrowed for short periods (a day or week at a time) in order to buy the long maturity bonds. The strategy made money as long as the short-term borrowing rate that Orange County paid was lower than the coupon (interest rate) of the Treasury bond. Rather than "no risk" or "low risk", the strategy had the huge risk of leverage. As each one-day or one-week loan matured, the lender had the right to raise the interest rate for the next loan or to refuse to lend at all. The short-term interest rate did, in fact, shoot higher and the fund lost approximately $1.7 billion.

As a final example, there's the Enron story of 2001. Enron has many lessons to teach. Histrionics aside, many employees claim they had fully invested their 401(k) retirement funds with

Enron stock. In hindsight, it's clear that was the worst possible investment choice. The employees who made this choice bet "the farm" (*i.e.*, both their retirement funds and their jobs) on Enron.

Why didn't these employees diversify their investments? Two reasons come to mind. First, it's human nature **not** to diversify since it's easier to put all your investments in one place. It's convenient to have just one basket for all the eggs. Second, many people don't understand the stock market. Enron's internal "public relations machine" may have hypnotized the employees into believing the stock would march forever upward. That may sound fatuous, but we've seen it happen at another large and successful company. Of course, the employees themselves bear responsibility for their decisions.

As a closing comment, we'd mentioned that all these stories had leverage as an element. The leverage story here is with Enron itself rather than the 401(k) plan. Almost all companies have some borrowing. Moderate leverage for businesses is not, in itself, destructive. Recall that Enron did **not** founder because of losses. Misrepresentation and possible fraud in the financial statements forced Enron to re-state its prior years' profits lower. But they were still profits! Not losses! Enron made a unique and critical business error by structuring its loans in a manner that guaranteed the firm's failure in the face of any "bad news" or "bad times". They were like an ocean liner that looks great above the water but sinks when it runs into a bad storm. Leverage sank Enron as other problems battered it.

Principles of Acceptable Investments

1. Stay within your risk tolerance
2. Be prepared to suffer a complete loss on any risky investment
3. Know what you are buying
4. All investments must be liquid
5. Make only those investments the values of which you can follow on a daily basis
6. Never borrow money to make investments
7. Diversify your investments

7

Efficient Markets

When financial pros say that a market is "efficient", they really mean there's no "easy way to make money". For example, if a trader can buy gold for $1600 per ounce in New York and sell immediately for $1610 in London, he/she will make a killing. (Typical size of such telephone-executed trades is greater than 10,000 ounces. Thus, this trader would make $100,000 simply for reading a screen that shows a New York offer of $1600 and a London bid of $1610 and then making two telephone calls.)

In reality, this trade never happens. Prices of gold between two locations never differ by so much simply because traders will jump on price differences. The act of buying at one (low) price in one city and selling at another (high) price in a second city forces the gold prices in the two cities to move closer to one another.

If a trader can buy gold (or anything else) at a certain price and then sell immediately at a known, higher price, then the trade is called an "arbitrage". We define "arbitrage" as "profit with zero risk". Arbitrage opportunities, when they exist, never last long because some trader somewhere will exploit it. In our example, the arbitrage disappears when the New York seller has no more gold to sell at $1600 per ounce (or when the London client has no more buying interest at $1610 per ounce).

Efficient markets are markets in which there are no arbitrage trades. The gold market is efficient since, as we said, the gold price difference between two cities is never significant. There are too many traders watching the prices all over the world who will "buy low and sell high" to wipe out even a $0.25 difference in price.

Let's discuss a trade that is **not** an arbitrage. Suppose our trader buys gold at $1600 per ounce in New York with the belief that the gold price will rise later that day. If the price does rise to $1610 and the trader sells, his/her profit is $100,000 on a 10,000-ounce trade. The profit is not an arbitrage, though, because the gold price could have fallen and produced a loss. Since there was no guarantee the trader would be able to sell at a higher price, the trader bore the "gold price risk" and, in this case, profited.

Most publicly recognized financial markets are efficient. Efficient markets are good! Individual investors should confine themselves to efficient markets for reasons we discuss at length later. Such markets protect us in that we will never pay "too much" for the stocks, bonds, or commodities we buy.

Efficient markets do not permit arbitrage trades. A related and more important observation is that **day-to-day price movements in efficient markets are random**. This "randomness" property may be the most important lesson of all investing. On average, we can say that almost all assets will appreciate over time (at different average growth rates). But we have absolutely no certainty that a specific stock (or bond or commodity) will grow in value over any time period. Neither is there any certainty that an entire market (such as the US stock market) will rise in value in the short or long terms.

Let's talk specifically about the (highly efficient) US stock market. Popular thought is that "professional investors" and "finance experts" can choose the stocks that will go up and avoid those that will fall or that such people can predict with some confidence whether the entire market will rise or fall. Not true … absolutely not true. Of all the tens of thousands of "professional money managers" over the years, there are probably less than five (Peter Lynch and Warren Buffett come to mind) that Wall Street could arguably claim "beat the market" consistently.

This phrase "beat the market" is a euphemism for "outperforming a monkey" (with no offense intended to the monkey). An investor (simian or otherwise) who chooses stocks completely randomly will "beat the market" half the time. Yet this is the standard against which professional equity investors measure themselves.

Our point here is not that money managers are dishonest or useless. They are not dishonest in that they will openly admit, when pressed, that they cannot reliably choose the winning stocks … even just 60% of the time. If they could, they'd always "beat the market" and nobody can show this record of accomplishment. Neither are these managers worthless since they can and will invest your money as you instruct them to do. If you want them to buy technology stocks, they'll buy technology stocks. The managers perform a service. It's critical to know, though, that they have no "magic touch" that will guarantee their performance is better than yours (or the market's).

We circle back in a later chapter to the topic of permitting professional managers to invest your money (*e.g*, mutual funds and hedge funds). For now, the point is that prices in efficient markets are random. Nobody, not even an "expert", knows where prices will go. When you think about it, there's a simple reason.

To see this reason, let's assume that, in fact, the experts

CAN predict which stock (or bond or commodity) prices will go up and which will go down. For example, let's say the IBM stock price is $200 today and the experts predict it will be $250 or higher in one year. What would happen? If these predictors truly believed their predictions, they'd buy the stock immediately! They wouldn't even announce the prediction. If the IBM stock price then does rise to $250, these investors will have earned a 25% return in one year (which is fantastic if one truly believes there is no uncertainty – and thus no risk – in the prediction).

So our first observation is that the experts would act on their own predictions if they truly believed them rather than announce predictions to the rest of us. Second, if these investors did act, their purchases would push the IBM stock price up beyond $200 per share. (Increased buying interest always pushes prices up while selling interest pushes them down.) These experts would keep buying until the price became close enough to the $250 prediction that the return on the investment is no longer sufficient.

In other words, market views ("predictions") and information impact the stock price immediately. The current price of any asset in an efficient market already reflects all market knowledge.

Market efficiency provides three lessons for investors. First, as we've discussed, nobody has any predictive ability for future market prices. Second, since the current price for any stock or bond or commodity embodies all market information, then this market price is the "fair" price. For example, the IBM stock price represents the consensus view of all investors (the skeptics, admirers, and disinterested parties). The "admirers" of IBM will have bought shares and, hence, pushed up the price. The "skeptics" of IBM will have sold shares short (which we'll explain in a later chapter) and, thus, pushed down the price. These two competing pressures on price become equal at the market price. That is, the market price is the "balance point" at which buyers and sellers cancel one another. A new investor who wants to buy IBM stock and has no idea what the price "should" be will pay the fair price. It's not like buying a used car!

Intriguingly, it is not just the "new investor" who does not know what the price of a share of stock (or bond or commodity) "should" be. Nobody knows, for example, what the IBM share price should be. The market price embodies much more information, analysis, and intelligence than any single expert can muster.

The third lesson of market efficiency is a variant of the first: nobody is a consistent, big winner. If your Uncle Cosmo or a guy on a radio commercial says he's doubled his money in six months, don't believe it. It **is** possible to buy a stock and have it double in six months. But nobody can achieve such success on most investments. If your investment portfolio gains 20% in one year, that's terrific. We don't gain wealth from winning bets but rather from healthy, compounded returns of buy-and-hold positions over many years.

Finally, what about "insider trading"? Are insiders (company officers or others with non-public knowledge) able to predict how a company's stock will move in the near term? Yes, and this observation contradicts one aspect of "market efficiency" that nobody has real predictive capability. For example, imagine that a company will announce its quarterly earnings on a Friday and that these earnings are much less than the investment community expects. The company's stock price will almost certainly fall on the news. While the stock price may then jump back to its original value over the following week or month, the one-day drop itself is "predictable".

To mitigate this "information advantage", there are laws and company policies that prohibit insiders from buying or selling stock or stock options **before** such announcements. Further, the company must report all trading activity in its stock and bonds of company officers to the public. If officers are net buyers or sellers of the stock, then, this knowledge becomes part of the "market intelligence" that sets the market price.

Unfortunately, there will always be illegal activity somewhere. An investment banker with non-public knowledge of a take-over may tell his/her friends or relatives to buy or sell certain stocks before the public has news of the event. But law enforcement does pursue and punish such transgressions. Though illegal insider trading does exist, the scale is sufficiently small so that it does not compromise the fundamental "fairness" of the market.

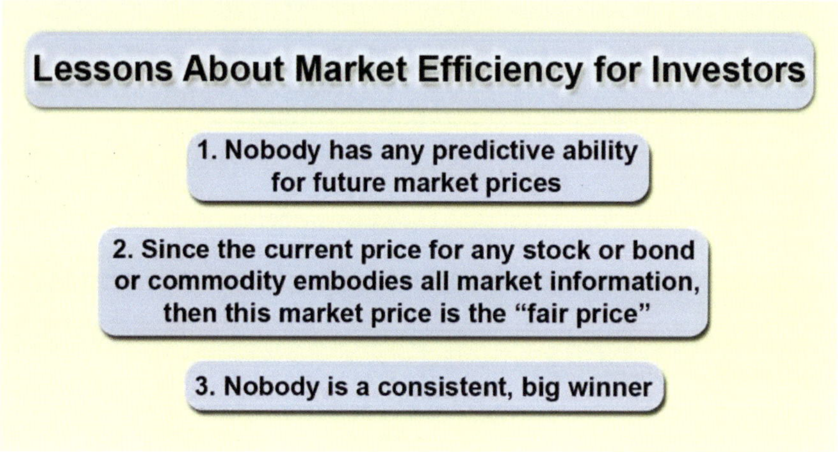

8

STOCKS

When we first begin to learn about investments, the array of choices can seem truly staggering. There are stocks, bonds, mutual funds, gold, and other commodities. We hear about futures trading, stock options, and IPOs ("initial public offerings"). The wealthy can select hedge funds for which the inscrutability of this phrase creates mystique.

This universe of potential investments is wide and confusing. There's good news. You can forget most of it. Only a small portion is necessary for individual investors. We advise you to limit yourself to stocks, bonds, and mutual funds. We discuss these three potential investments in detail in this and the following two chapters. Actually, mutual funds require little comment once you understand stocks and bonds. In mutual funds you simply pool your money with other investors and pay somebody else to buy stocks or bonds on your behalf. A further chapter also adds explanations of many other assets and investment products for curious readers.

Businesses need money. That's a fairly obvious statement. Though all businesses differ, most need property and a building for the place of business as well as equipment. Virtually all companies need investors to supply the money to start or expand activities. If the investor is a bank, then the cash infusion will be a loan. The company must re-pay the loan at a designated time (the "loan maturity") and pay interest every three months, typically, until this maturity. Similarly, a business issues bonds as a form of borrowing. Like a loan, a bond requires the company (the borrower) to re-pay the principal at a specific maturity date and pay interest at regular intervals until maturity. We discuss bonds in more detail in the next chapter.

Stockholders Are Owners

The stock (also known as the "equity") of a company is not a loan. Stockholders pay their money to become <u>owners</u> of the firm. As owners, the stockholders control the company. In practice, the stockholders elect directors to serve on the "board of directors". This board hires the senior executives who, in turn, run the operation on a day-to-day basis. A firm's profit is the total revenue it earns by selling its products minus all expenses and taxes. Many, but not all, companies pay dividends to the stockholders (or "shareholders") in order to distribute immediately a portion of this profit. The board of directors, which should always act solely on behalf of the shareholders,* decides whether or not to pay a dividend each quarter. Many boards oppose dividend payments in the belief that it is best for shareholders to re-invest all profits in the business.

The most important, single aspect of stock investing is that you are an owner of the company. Whatever is good for the company is good for your investment. It is just as if you and some friends got together to establish a restaurant. Let's say there are five of you who make equal contributions of $10,000. This initial $50,000 secures a lease for the building and purchases equipment and renovation. With such a small business, the five of you are your own board of directors. You jointly decide whom to hire to run the restaurant. If the business fails, then you shut down, sell the remaining assets (*i.e.*, kitchen equipment), and distribute the residual cash to the owners. You cannot lose more than your original investment.

If this restaurant thrives, on the other hand, the investment will benefit the owners in two ways. First, you will receive a

* More correctly, the Board acts exclusively in the interests of shareholders unless the business is at the brink of failure. In this distressed circumstance, the Board may also have fiduciary duty to guard the interests of creditors.

fraction of the restaurant's profits, which will be the same fraction as your ownership, as dividend payments unless you and your friends jointly decide to use some or all profits to expand the size of the business. Second, you'll be able to sell your share of the restaurant for more than your $10,000 investment.

That's the essence of stock ownership. If the company fails, you'll lose substantially (though never more than your investment). If the company succeeds, you'll win by receiving dividend payments and watching the value of your stock increase. The dividends are typically much less than any gain or loss of the stock value.

The restaurant example emphasizes the point that stockholders are owners of the company. Unlike this small business illustration, though, owning the stock of a large company such as General Electric (GE) has the advantage that investors can follow daily the value of their partial ownership. If you own 100 shares of GE and the day's stock price is $20 per share, your ownership stake is worth $2,000. (For GE, 100 shares is about 0.000001% of the roughly 10 billion total outstanding shares of the company.)

Market Price is the "Fair Price"

If today's GE stock price is $20, it may easily move to $21 or $19 tomorrow. This observation raises the two related questions of how the market "knows" the value of GE and how this value can really change so much in just a day. Good questions! We have no good answers! The truth is that nobody knows how much GE is worth. If we knew with certainty how profitable the company would be over the next thirty years (or longer), then we'd be able to calculate a "correct" value. But nobody, including GE executives, has any certainty regarding *any* future earnings.

It may surprise you that we cannot simply add up the value of all of GE's assets and then subtract the value of all liabilities (the money it owes to lenders). As individuals, this is how we get our own net worth. For a company, this difference between assets and liabilities is the "book value". The "market value" (market stock price multiplied by the number of the company's shares of stock) is generally greater than this book value. You can say that a business is often "worth more than the sum of its parts". Or, we express the same idea by claiming that GE will make more money for shareholders by remaining in business and earning profits than by selling all assets and paying off its debt.

In one sense, it seems that the market price of a stock (such as GE at $20) cannot be "correct" since there is no verbal argument or explanation for this particular value. It is merely on one day the price at which the number of buyers equals the number of sellers. Philosophically, there is no "correct price" for GE stock since we cannot know the future. The only reality is the level at which others will sell the stock to you (if you wish to buy) or the level at which others will buy from you (if you wish to sell). So, there is actually deep meaning in the statement that "the market price is the right price".

Fortunately, the US has efficient markets for the stock of virtually all public companies of reasonable size. As chapter 7 on Efficient Markets noted, in such markets one always pays the "fair price" since the market price is known to all and is the level at which all trades take place. Avoid inefficient markets since you have no assurance you are paying or receiving the "fair price" when you buy or sell. Hence, don't buy into the restaurant with your friends as an investment. Small restaurant businesses do not constitute an efficient market. Unless you're a professional in this business, consider such a venture to be "recreation", "entertainment", or "a hobby" and do not count this activity as part of your investment portfolio.

Choosing Stock Investments

Stock values in efficient markets can go up or down. Investing experts and professionals have no idea which stocks will shoot up and which will decline. If you're comfortable with the level of risk, which stocks should you buy? That's the fun part! Buy what you want to own. Buy what you're proud to own. Buy a company in whose business you want to take part.

For example, how would you choose between IBM and GE? Ask yourself which company you'd rather own. If you've had a particularly favorable (or unfavorable) experience with one of the company's products, then buy (or don't buy) that firm's stock. Any other type of strong feeling about a company is a reasonable basis for such an investment choice. You may admire (or hold in low esteem) a company's management, for example. If you eat at McDonald's often, then you must enjoy the food. Buy the stock, too. On the contrary, if you're one of those people for whom deriding "fast food" is intellectual sport, don't buy McDonald's stock.

Let's emphasize that none of these thoughts will make your equity investment outperform the market (*i.e.*, do better than other stocks). But building in your preferences won't hurt, either. Investing with your own tastes, opinions, and prejudices will make the exercise more personal and fun. Have fun! It's your money! You'll enjoy your McDonald's meal more knowing "you own the company". When you board a jet, you'll look out the window to see if the engines are GE's or those of the "hated competitors" (Pratt & Whitney or Rolls-Royce).

You can make your own personal case for owning or not owning virtually any company in our economy. If you have young children, you may appreciate Disney movies, television, theme parks, and radio. Buy the company, then, and become one of the people who provide these products. Consider the healthcare field. Drug companies spend billions on research to cure diseases and otherwise improve the quality of our lives. How much more noble can a company's mission be? When you buy the stock of a drug company, you are embracing this mission and making it your own.

Some people take the opposing view and argue that drug companies are "bad" because they wish to profit from their investments. Let's leave aside the implied debate between capitalism and socialism and make this suggestion. If you don't like the drug companies' profit motive, then buy the company and work to change it from within. Vote your shares whenever possible to reduce the company's profitability. Unless you own a huge percentage of the stock, though, you won't likely succeed directly. But, you can certainly take any dividends or stock appreciation you receive and donate these gains to a charity that helps others buy drugs. With this effective activist strategy, you will immediately reduce the profitability of a portion of this drug company (*i.e.*, the portion you own). Sounds like a joke, and maybe it is, but it's also true!

The larger point here is that equity investing makes you a part of each company you own and it makes you a part of the entire economy. Not only do your decisions matter, but you will find yourself learning much more about how the economy works. You'll be surprised how much and how quickly you'll learn when economic and legislative news directly affects your investments. Newspaper articles on seemingly tiresome subjects (*e.g.*, Intel's growth strategy) become fascinating!

Buy and Hold !

The two key strategies for managing your stock portfolio are "buy and hold" and "diversification". The first of these suggestions simply advises that you keep stocks you buy for very long periods of time. If you buy a stock at $50 per share and it rises to $60, you may be tempted to sell in order to "realize your profit". Don't sell! Leave the stock alone. Because the stock market is efficient, neither you nor anybody else know that this stock value is more likely to fall than to continue rising. If this value of $60 seems high to you, then don't buy more.

Let's say, though, that your $50 stock falls to $40. This is the situation in which some investors get cold feet and sell the stock before it falls further. Some advisors will even say "cut your losses short and let the winners run". Again, in efficient markets, a stock that falls to $40 is **not** more likely to continue falling than it is to bounce back. Instead of selling, many investors would buy more of this stock that's fallen to $40 from $50. Financial advisors have a saying for this philosophy as well: "If you like it at $50, you should love it at $40!"

The implied advice of these two preceding paragraphs to stop buying stock that rises and to buy more of stock that falls is not strictly logical. The market price of a stock in efficient markets is the "right price". It doesn't matter if the stock has been trending up or down. The complete irrelevance of trends in stock prices is highly counter-intuitive. The true wisdom of "buy and hold" is that investors should almost always be buyers. Put your money in the market and make it work. Spend very little of your time wondering when to take money out. Since the market is efficient, you cannot "pick the winners" in the stock market and you cannot "time" the market. So place your money in stocks of companies you want to own and keep it there.

This suggestion raises the question of when do you sell your stock? The goal is not simply to pass stock ownership to your heirs. Quite simply, sell your stock when you need the money or when the stock no longer suits your investment goals. For example, if you need substantial cash to buy a house or car or make tuition payments, then you may need to sell investments. That's normal. One reason to build wealth is to have cash for such expenses. Alternatively, it may be that you no longer "like" the stock you own. It's not the price of the stock that drives this decision. Rather, you may decide you no longer wish to own the company. Perhaps the company merged with another and now has a new business plan that you are no longer "proud" to espouse. Or you may be closer to retirement (and diminution of income) and no longer want the relatively high risk of the stock.

There certainly will come a time to sell your stock investments. Plan to hold stock investments for many years, though. You'll gain nothing with short-term trading while adding to the workload of managing your money. Short-term trading also costs money in the form of paying the "bid-offer spread". In liquid markets, this difference between dealer bid price and dealer offer price is small, so this particular loss is not large unless short-term trading is truly excessive. In illiquid markets the bid-offer difference is significant and provides yet another reason to avoid illiquid stocks and other investments.

Diversify the Portfolio

One of the simplest investment errors is to put all or most of your money into one stock. Though stocks of different companies do have different levels of risk, any stock can double in a year and any stock can fall to a horrendously low level. In efficient markets, nobody knows what will happen to any stock or group of stocks. If you concentrate your investments in a small number of stocks, you leave yourself open to catastrophic loss.

In a prior chapter we emphasized that any risky asset can fall to zero value and that you should only invest money in such assets that you can afford to lose. Use risk-free investments for that portion of your investment portfolio that you cannot afford to lose. Having said that, it remains a good idea to minimize the chance of losing all your money in risky investments!

Consider a simple example. Let's say, quite reasonably, that IBM and GE stock have the same expected return. If we put all our money into IBM or all our money into GE, then we'll have this expected return as well as very small probabilities of losing all our money or, conversely, doubling our money within a year.

Instead of this concentration, let's now think about splitting our investment between IBM and GE. The expected return of this two-stock portfolio remains unchanged, but the probability of total loss (already small!) falls tremendously. To lose our entire investment, we'd need to see the stocks of both IBM and GE become worthless in the same period. This dual catastrophe is much less likely than the demise of either IBM or GE separately. Of course, the portfolio of IBM and GE stocks is also less likely to double than either stock by itself. So, the "diversification" to two stocks maintains the expected return while reducing the chance of huge losses or gains.

Common wisdom in the US stock market is that an investor needs investments of roughly equal amount in as many as thirty stocks to be "fully diversified". With such a portfolio, your gains or losses will be similar to the stock market as a whole. In our view, this number is too high. It's difficult to know and "believe in" so many different companies. Further, the mathematical argument that leads to the thirty-stock diversification threshold makes an assumption that we consider to be inappropriate for unleveraged investors. Simply speaking, investors do not seek to minimize their risk in the manner the argument presumes.

Though somewhat arbitrary, we consider ten to fifteen stocks as appropriate diversification for an equity portfolio. This size is small enough so that an investor can "know" the companies and large enough to avert staggering losses. The companies should differ somewhat from each other. For example, it's prudent to count two US steel producers as being "one company" for the sake of measuring your diversification. If one steel manufacturer declares bankruptcy, there's a good chance the other will also in the same timeframe.

Early in your investing career you may not have this much diversification. This "ramp-up period" is unavoidable. If you're primarily an equity investor, keep about 20% in cash (*e.g.*, a risk-free money market fund) and buy new stocks as time goes on. Don't buy more of a stock you already own until there are at least (approximately) five separate companies in your portfolio. Let the diversification increase over time. You'll have the opportunity to learn about more corporations.

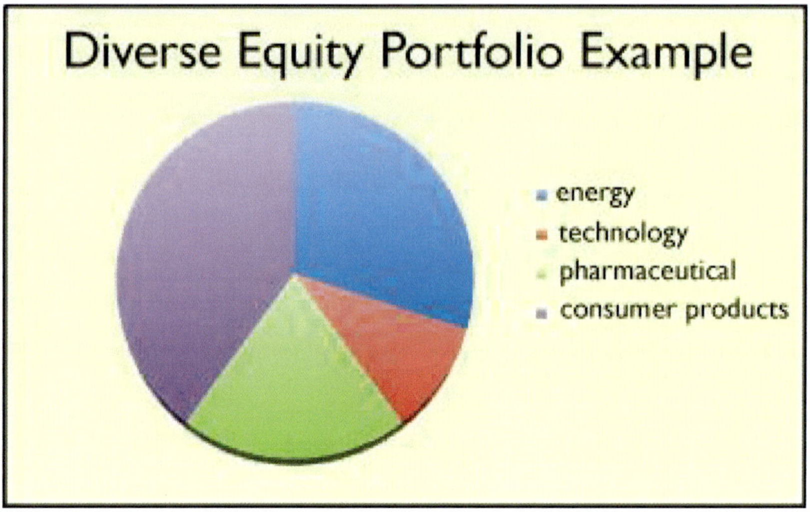

Achilles Heel: Board of Directors

The backbone of our free market, capitalist economy is the freedom and ability to create and invest in lawful businesses without the participation of government. It's possible that even Karl Marx would agree that "workers" (which I'll transform to "all people") can now own the "means of production" if they choose. But when so many "workers" own a company, the challenge is creating a practical mechanism to run the firm as the owners desire. Some public companies have millions of shareholders!

The mechanism in place for US public companies appears to be better than any alternative. Each company has a board of directors that consists of men and women the stockholders elect. Each share of stock represents one vote. Hence, if any single investor owns 51% of the outstanding stock, he/she effectively controls the company.

This board of directors (or, "board") then hires the company's senior management. For example, the chief executive officer (CEO) is the highest-ranking employee. He/she supervises the firm's operation on a day-to-day, month-to-month basis and performs and/or delegates all activities necessary for the company's short-term and long-term success. The board continually monitors the CEO's performance and plans for the company's future. Though the board decides many points, there are several issues on which the shareholders must vote directly. These issues include the issuance of more stock, agreement to acquisition or merger, and appointment of auditors.

So, on paper, it sounds good. Even though we think of the CEO as the most powerful person in a company, he/she is only an employee and does not have the right to make decisions with which the majority of owners would disagree. So the owners elect the board of directors to manage the CEO to assure that he/she acts in their best interests. The true situation is not so clear, though! Company employees themselves sit on the board and the CEO often serves as the chairman! These "company directors" may constitute a majority of the board. Even if a minority, though, this employee presence on the board diminishes the board's independence and oversight. The nonemployee, "independent" directors must be nearly unanimous to thwart the will of the employee directors.

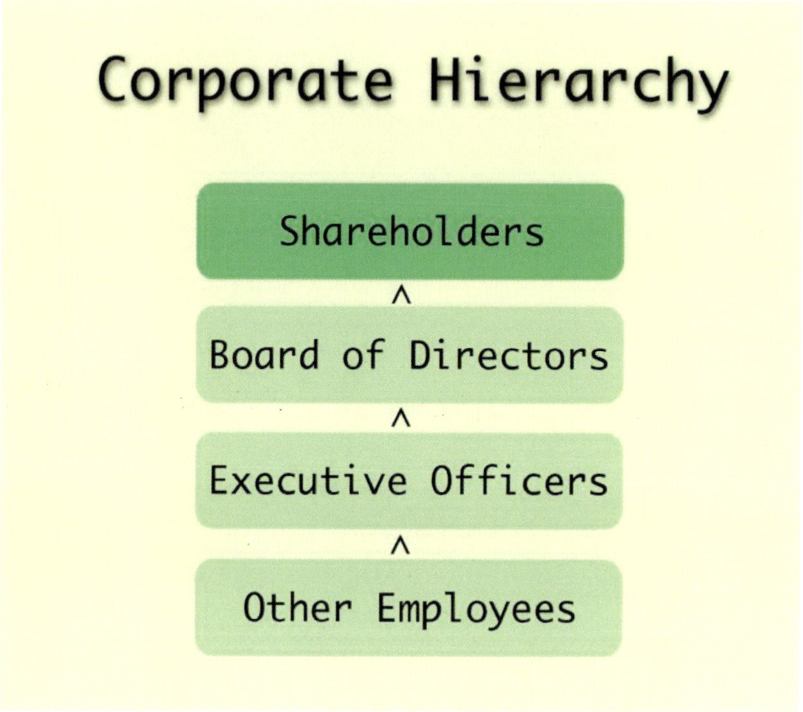

People are human. Ideally, the employees' goals and interests should be precisely those of the owners so that the board would be merely an advisory committee. That is, fill the board with experienced and intelligent people who will debate strategy good-naturedly and detect honest errors and oversights of the employees. While employees, like owners, do want the company to succeed, they also desire high compensation, job security, and personal expense budgets that may not be in the owners' interest. Thus, a board of directors must be vigilant in dealing with this inherent conflict of interests between employees and stockholders.

Again, the CEO is just an employee. But as chairman of the board, he/she also supposedly represents the stockholders. The existence of employee directors is antithetical to sound business practice and common sense. The argument in favor of employee directors is that the senior employees understand the business best, which is undoubtedly true, and that corporate governance benefits from their specialized knowledge and expertise. Our rebuttal is that senior employees can certainly advise and make recommendations to the board without being members of the board.

A reasonable counter-argument to the view that employees should not serve as directors is that stockholders have the right to give the CEO this type of power. Since the stockholders elect the directors, they certainly have the right to elect employees or anybody else. Unfortunately, this argument brings us to another problem. Stockholder votes are highly ineffective. Many stockholders fail to vote their shares. Such uncast ballots may become votes for the position that the board recommends. This predicament is even worse than our political elections! Imagine if we counted every vote of non-participating adult citizens for the incumbent! Our politicians would leave office only when we carry their bodies on stretchers! When a board of directors proposes a new member to the stockholders (to replace a retiring member, for example), it is virtually assured that this new member will "win election".

So, the sad truth is that boards of directors are largely immune to the will of the stockholders in typical companies with widespread ownership. It gets worse! Outside (independent) directors attend board meetings only 3-4 times per year and may receive a stipend for their participation that provides a faulty incentive. Since directors are generally prominent business and academic leaders, a low stipend (such as $20,000 per annum) would not provide a financial incentive to exert great energy as directors given competing time commitments. A higher stipend (such as $200,000 per annum) for the limited work of a director, on the other hand, may give the director the incentive to maintain the board position. A director who stirs trouble by opposing too strenuously the views of other board members may find himself/herself removed!

This long diatribe paints quite a bleak picture. Fortunately, there are two aspects that brighten the landscape. First, both employee and outside directors are almost universally people of integrity. While there may be too little financial incentive to serve diligently on the board (or too much incentive to remain on the board), the directors have their honor and reputations to protect. Prominent people who have both wealth and experience are loath to play starring roles in a business scandal. True malfeasance on a board of directors is exceedingly rare.

When it does occur, it's likely to involve an employee director. The greater risk is stupidity, rather than impropriety, of the directors. Always look for intelligence, accomplishment, and experience on the board of directors of companies you buy.

The second reason for optimism in the face of perverse incentives of corporate governance is the public market itself. The market understands that the board cannot shield stockholders from an inept or unethical management team. Therefore, the market scrutinizes the management team itself rather than the board. If the market sees management performing inimically to the interests of the shareholders, it drives the stock price down. A plunging stock price gets everybody's attention! Even more than advising on long-term strategy, the single most important role of the board of directors is to ensure that all public disclosures are accurate and complete. With good disclosure, the market price of the stock will give the board the information it needs to evaluate management team performance.

Hostile Takeovers and Poison Pills

All in all, then, corporate governance works due to "market discipline" and accurate public disclosure. Still, we can't resist launching one more salvo against the current system. The financial world defines a "hostile takeover" as company A making a bid to buy company B without the consent of the board of directors of company B. What's the real problem here that earns the adjective "hostile"? If we own stock in company B, we encourage *anybody* to bid for our shares above the current market value as is the custom for all takeovers. We may choose not to sell, but why should the board prevent company A from bidding for our shares?

Of course, the board may truly believe that, despite the market price of company B stock, company A's bid is not adequate. Thus, the board may feel that stockholders will fare better over the long term by rejecting the takeover. That's quite possible, but bear in mind that all directors may lose their jobs! For employee directors especially, there's a huge conflict in a takeover between their interests and those of the stockholders. The real hostility in a "hostile" takeover is the ill will with which some directors may treat their stockholders' interests.

While a board's recommendation to shareholders that it reject a takeover may be principled, a board's active discouragement of takeover interest is incredibly abusive. A "poison pill" is any measure a board of directors adopts the intent of which is to discourage potential buyers. For example, the provision may state that, upon an outside investor's purchase of 10% or more of outstanding stock without takeover "recommendation" of the board, all remaining shareholders will receive a new and valuable claim on the company. This type of measure makes acquisition more expensive than it should be.

Think of the big picture here! As a stockholder, you *want*

other investors to be potential buyers of your company whether it's 100 shares at a time or 51% of all outstanding shares. Buying interest pushes up the value of the stock. Any effort to *eliminate* potential buyers must push the stock price down somewhat. That should not be the goal of the board!

Once again, though, optimism reigns here. The stock market does police this sort of problem. The market sees "poison pills" and reflects these ill-advised corporate actions in the stock price. If you have the chance, vote your shares against poison pills. If one of your companies enacts a poison pill, consider selling your shares if you agree with us that management and the board do not share your values.

Exotic Stocks

Some companies sell "preferred stock" to public investors. Relative to regular stock (also known as "common stock"), preferred stock generally has two advantages. First, it provides high dividend payments. Common stock often has no dividend or a very low dividend rate such as 1% - 3% per annum. Preferred stock dividends are typically in the range 5% - 15%. Second, if the company files for bankruptcy, preferred stock investors have preference over common stockholders. That is, when the bankruptcy court sells all assets, the proceeds go first to lenders and bondholders, second to preferred stockholders, and finally to common stockholders.

The disadvantage of preferred stock is that it does not confer ownership upon the investor. The preferred stockholder cannot vote on corporate decisions. The common stockholders are the owners. Since preferred stockholders are not owners, they do not benefit when the company profits increase. Preferred stock really resembles bonds of the company much more than it does common stock. In fact, preferred stock is equivalent in many respects to subordinated bonds, which we discuss under the heading of "Exotic Bonds" in chapter 9 on "Bonds".

Another instrument, "convertible preferred stock", gives the investor preferred stock – with the high dividend and preference under bankruptcy – as well as the ability to profit from the company's success. It's a mixture of lending and ownership. Convertible preferred stock is preferred stock that the holder has the right to exchange for a fixed amount of common stock. It's always cheaper to buy the common stock directly. Thus, the preferred stockholder pays more in the hope that the higher dividend of preferred stock will be worth this premium cost.

Both preferred stock and convertible preferred stock are "acceptable investments" since they generally have good liquidity and price transparency. There's no strong reason to avoid preferred stock if you understand that this instrument is essentially a subordinated bond and if you know how conversion features, if any, work. In other words, preferred stock as an investment gives added complexity with which you must be comfortable.

9

BONDS

As we noted earlier, a company may borrow from a bank in the form of a "bank loan". The company may also issue bonds in order to borrow from other investors. Bonds generally have a "face value", or denomination, of $1,000. The investor will typically, but not always, pay approximately this face value to buy the bond. The borrower (*i.e.*, the company that issues the bond) must re-pay the face value to the bond investor on the bond's stated maturity date. The bond also pays interest to the investor at a stated "coupon" every six months. The bond really does function just like a loan. A primary difference between bonds and bank loans is that non-bank investors are able to buy and sell the bonds.

The bonds and stock of a company differ in many respects. While the stockholder is an owner of the company, the bondholder is a lender. The company's board of directors runs the company for the benefit of stockholders. An independent "trustee" – usually a bank – monitors the company's adherence to its bond obligations and will sue the company, if necessary, to protect the bondholders' interests.

Investment Risk of Bonds

The risk of a bond investment in, say, GE is easier to understand than the risk of an equity (stock) investment. The bond will either pay the stated interest (coupon) and principal (face value) or it won't. Bankruptcy prior to bond maturity represents the only situation in which the borrower would not pay interest and principal. Since bankruptcies are rare, it is highly likely the bond investor will receive all payments. There is a very small probability that the investor will not receive such payments. In this bankruptcy event, the bondholder often receives about half of what the company owes after extended litigation. This "recovery amount", though, can certainly be much less.

So, the bond "risk profile" is fairly simple. With high probability, the investor gets all stated payments. With very small probability, the investor receives an unknown (lesser) recovery amount. The risk profile for the equity investor is far more uncertain. As we discussed in the preceding section, the stock value will go up or down in a manner that is quite unpredictable. All we can say is that if a company's business prospers beyond expectations, the stock value is likely to increase. If the company declares bankruptcy, the stock value will decrease dramatically and will most often become worthless. (In bankruptcy, leftover money of any kind goes first to bank lenders and bondholders before stockholders. The lenders have "priority". Stockholders receive nothing unless lenders recoup their full investment.)

Bond investors appreciate this vast difference in risk profiles. Bonds have much less risk than stocks. Since expected return of any investment increases with the risk, bonds have much lower expected return than stocks. The interest rate (coupon) of a typical bond is only 1-3% higher than the comparable risk-free rate and depends strongly on the risk of the borrower. For example, if a US Treasury bond pays a 5% interest rate, the corporate bond rate may be 6-8%. Expected returns of stock ownership are typically 10% and higher.

When a business performs well or poorly, both bondholders and stockholders feel a gain or loss. That is, when a company does well, it is less likely to declare bankruptcy and its stock will likely rise in value. In this sense, the interests of bondholders and stockholders are "aligned". But there are other ways in which the interests of these two classes of investors are not aligned. For example, when a company issues more bonds it increases its leverage and makes its own bankruptcy more likely. That's bad for bondholders but good for stockholders in that the extra leverage increases the likelihood that the stock value will increase (even though it also increases bankruptcy risk). Conversely, a company that issues more equity will hurt the interests of stockholders while helping that of bondholders.

Types of Bonds

In terms of borrowers in the United States, there are three types of bonds. Companies, such as GE in the example above, issue "corporate" bonds. The US government sells "government bonds" which we also call "Treasury" bonds. Finally, other governmental entities – such as states, cities, villages, *et cetera* – borrow money with "municipal" (or "muni") bonds. Corporate, US government, and municipal bonds are similar in that they are loans with stated coupons and maturity dates. It makes sense, though, to label them separately for a few reasons.

First, market professionals consider Treasury bonds to be risk-free. While one might argue philosophically that nothing is perfectly risk-free, the market defines the "risk-free rate" for a specific maturity as the interest rate of this maturity's Treasury bond. (The counter-argument to the philosopher might be that we'll all have bigger problems than our bond yields if the US government stops paying its debts.) Treasury bills (or "T-bills") are essentially Treasury bonds with maturities of one year or less. Treasury notes are just Treasury bonds with maturities of two to ten years. Interest income of Treasury bonds is exempt from state taxation.

Second, municipal bonds deserve a distinct category since tax considerations drive this market. Municipal bonds may be either "taxable" or "tax-exempt". Investors in tax-exempt municipal bonds generally need not pay federal, state, or local income tax on the bond interest assuming the investor resides in the same state as the municipal issuer. As a consequence, the market price of a tax-exempt bond will be higher than a comparable taxable bond.

Finally, liquidity varies considerably between these three markets. Treasury market liquidity is outstanding. You'll always find competitive bid and offer prices for Treasury bonds. Daily prices are available in many newspapers and websites. Corporate bond liquidity is irregular. Large bond issues of well-known companies such as AT&T and Disney will have reasonable liquidity (though not nearly as high as Treasury bonds). Smaller bond issues are often illiquid. As a rule, municipal bond liquidity is lacking. Municipal issue sizes tend to be small and the tax considerations segment the investor universe.

Credit Ratings

We commented that the bond risk profile is straightforward. The bond will "default" (*i.e.*, fail to pay full principal and interest) with a small probability that we call the "default probability". With high probability, on the other hand, the bond will make all payments. Bonds of different companies have very different default probabilities. An excellent measure of a particular company's default probability is the bond's "credit rating". There are private firms that the market calls "credit rating agencies" the most prominent of which are Moody's Investors Service, Inc., Standard & Poor's Ratings Services, Fitch Ratings, and DBRS, Inc. These agencies have long histories of assigning ratings to advise bond investors of default risk. Moody's, Standard & Poor's, Fitch, and DBRS all have good track records in identifying high-risk and low-risk corporate and municipal bonds. There is, however, no assurance that the ratings are "correct". Rather, ratings are, ideally, unbiased and expert opinions on the level of default risk.

The highest credit rating, which implies the lowest default probability, for a bond is "triple-**A**" (also written as "**Aaa**" or "**AAA**"). As default risk increases, the associated bond ratings change as we show in the table below down to "double-**C**".

Below double-**C**, a bond is in default (at which point opinions on the default likelihood are irrelevant). For historical and, yet, arbitrary reasons, finance professionals call ratings of triple-**B** through triple-**A** "investment grade". By the same token, the ratings of double-**B** down through double-**C** are "speculative grade" and also "junk". So, "junk bond" just means a bond with a credit rating of double-**B** or below.

Credit Rating	Also Known As	
Triple-A	Aaa	AAA
Double-A	Aa	AA
Single-A	A	A
Triple-**B**	**Baa**	**BBB**
Double-**B**	**Ba**	**BB**
Single-**B**	**B**	**B**
Triple-C	Caa	CCC
Double-C	Ca	CC

Triple-**A** bonds have extremely low default risk. Default of a bond with this rating is essentially "unthinkable". A triple-**A** bond is not completely "risk-free" since we still consider debts of the US government to have smaller default risk. The default of any investment grade bond is rare. For example, one reason for the shock of the 2001 Enron fiasco is that this company enjoyed a triple-**B** credit rating until the week prior to its bankruptcy filing. (We specifically leave out of this discussion the poor performance of ratings on "structured products" beginning in 2006. Our focus here is on corporate and municipal bonds for which ratings performance has remained acceptable.)

Bond Yield

These credit ratings are extremely important for bond investors. Never buy a bond unless you know the bond rating. Bonds with low ratings (for example, junk bonds) are not necessarily bad investments. Such bonds simply have higher default probabilities than more highly rated bonds. That means there's more risk and the bond's investment "yield" must be higher to compensate you for the extra risk.

The bond yield is just the interest rate you earn for buying the bond. If the market price of the bond is "par" (which means you pay $1,000 for a bond with face value of $1,000), then the yield is the coupon rate of the bond. But the bond price often differs from par. Bond prices change from day to day just as stock prices do. Unlike stock investors, though, bond investors think in terms of yield rather than price. When the bond price rises from one week to the next, the bond's yield falls since the buyer must pay more this week than last week for the same principal and interest (coupon) payments. There are mathematical equations that can give you the bond's yield when you know the price, coupon rate, and maturity. Fortunately, listings of bond prices almost always do these yield calculations for you. If your broker suggests you buy a particular bond, he/she will provide the bond's current yield.

Efficient Markets in Bonds ?

In purchasing a bond, then, you must know the credit rating and the current yield. Taking high risk – as with a junk bond – is perfectly reasonable if the bond yield is sufficiently high to compensate for the risk. In fact, "junk bond risk" is generally much less than equity risk. Newspaper and television personalities love to harumph and grimace when they speak of junk bonds, but the risks of most such securities are not excessive.

Of course, the difficulty lies in knowing when a bond yield is "sufficiently high" for the default risk. If bond markets are efficient (see chapter 7 on Efficient Markets), then the current bond price implies a yield that is the market consensus of "sufficiently high" yield. In other words, the market price is the "right price". Unfortunately, one cannot assume that corporate bond markets are efficient as one often can for the stocks of the same companies. In purchasing individual corporate bonds, it is best to buy only those bonds with issue sizes of $500 million and higher. This large size is the best indicator that you will find a buyer for the bond if you wish to sell prior to maturity.

The market in Treasury bonds is highly efficient. You will always "pay the right price" for Treasury debt instruments. The price transparency of this market is high. Municipal bond markets, on the other hand, are inefficient. There is significant risk you will pay "too much" for any bond you purchase and that you will receive "too little" if you sell the bond before maturity. In our view, municipal bonds are not "acceptable investments".

Choosing Bond Investments

In choosing a bond investment, a primary consideration is the liquidity of the market for the bond as we've just discussed. Buy only liquid bonds since you're more likely to lose money by paying too much and selling too cheaply with illiquid bonds. A second significant point is the bond's credit rating. If none of the credit rating agencies have rated the bond, then go no further. Don't even consider the investment. Use the rating from one of these agencies to understand the level of risk. If you are comfortable only with bonds that almost certainly will not default, then buy bonds with ratings of double-**A** and triple-**A**. If, conversely, you're willing to take risk in order to earn higher yield and you realize at least one of the bonds in your portfolio is likely to default over the next five years or so, then buy bonds with ratings as low as single-**B**.

Averaged over a period of many years, high-risk bonds will give you higher return than low-risk bonds. A high-risk bond portfolio will have defaults, but the higher yields on the non-defaulted bonds will offset the default losses. But don't ignore this warning. There's no guarantee that your particular high-risk bond portfolio will perform better than a low-risk portfolio over any time period. With high-risk bonds, you accept the risk that your portfolio may have more defaults than the average. On average, you'll do better with high-risk bonds. But your particular investments may do worse or better. That's the way risk works.

Once you've limited yourself to liquid bonds with the credit ratings that make you comfortable, the final consideration is your choice of borrowers (*i.e.*, bond issuers). In picking stock investments, we noted that stockholders are owners of the companies. You should buy stock of companies you want to own. Similarly, when you buy a bond, you become a lender to the company that issues the bond. Choose companies to which you want to lend. In effect, the company will take the money you've given and invest it in the firm's business. If you buy McDonald's bonds, you'll help build more of their restaurants. Buying a pharmaceutical company's bonds supports research for new drugs.

Treasury bonds are risk-free. An investor who purchases Treasuries is certain to receive the stated principal and interest and understands that the investment yield is relatively small as payment for this certainty. The main consideration for this investor is the Treasury bond maturity. Choose the maturity to match the approximate time in the future when you'll want the cash back. If you want "certain" funds for retirement in thirty years, buy a thirty-year Treasury bond. If you're saving for college tuition payments two years hence, buy a two-year Treasury note. You'll be able to sell Treasury bonds prior to maturity at any time, but it's to your advantage to let the bonds mature rather than sell them since the market price of non-matured bonds may fall below par.

Exotic Bonds

Bonds are a straightforward concept. They represent loans to the bond issuers. Finance people are adept at taking simple ideas and adding complexity. Subordinated and convertible bonds are two examples. A borrower's subordinated bond has higher risk, higher yield, and a lower credit rating than the same borrower's normal ("senior") bond. The greater risk arises from inferior priority that subordinated bondholders receive in bankruptcy. The senior bondholders have first claim to repayment in bankruptcy court while the subordinated investors stand second. It's reasonable to assume subordinated bondholders receive zero recovery when the borrower defaults.

Convertible bonds, which themselves may be senior or subordinated, give the bondholder the right to exchange the bonds at a future time for a fixed number of shares of the stock of the borrower. An investor in such a convertible bond hopes the stock will rise in value so that he/she profits from the equity price movement. For example, imagine the investor pays $1,000 for the bond and has the right to convert this bond into 20 shares of stock. If the original stock value is $30 per share, the investor would not choose to convert the bond to stock immediately since 20 shares of the stock is worth $600 which is far less than the cost of the bond. If the stock doubles in value to $60 per share, though, then the conversion makes sense since 20 shares of the stock would be worth $1,200. Convertible bond investors seek this potential gain in stock value without the potential loss of a fall in the stock value. It sounds like a good idea, but realize that the investor pays for this convertible feature by accepting a low bond coupon. If the stock never rises as one hopes, then the yield of the bond is much less than it should be for the borrower's default risk.

Both subordinated and convertible bonds are generally unacceptable investments for the individual investor since the liquidity is often inadequate. Thus, the markets for these securities are not efficient and there is substantial likelihood of losing value in the purchase and sale.

Wisdom of Bond Investments

Treasury bonds of all maturities are excellent investments for individual investors who desire essentially zero risk for all or part of their portfolios. The liquidity and price transparency of Treasuries are unbeatable. Individual corporate and municipal bonds, on the other hand, are less compelling. Our strong advice that individual investors restrict themselves to liquid markets eliminates all municipal and most corporate bonds. The remaining liquid corporate bonds have only one advantage relative to Treasuries: the yield may be a few percentage points higher. This small gain is arguably not worth the individual investor's effort to choose and follow a corporate bond portfolio.

Of course, *somebody* should buy bonds. Individuals who consider stock to be too risky, but don't want completely risk-free investments, are natural buyers of (liquid) corporate bonds. Professional investors overcome the "low return" of bonds by leveraging their positions (*i.e.*, borrowing money to buy the bonds). Leverage magnifies risk and return. Hence, corporate bonds are more suitable for professional investors rather than individuals who are better served with Treasury securities.

10

MUTUAL FUNDS

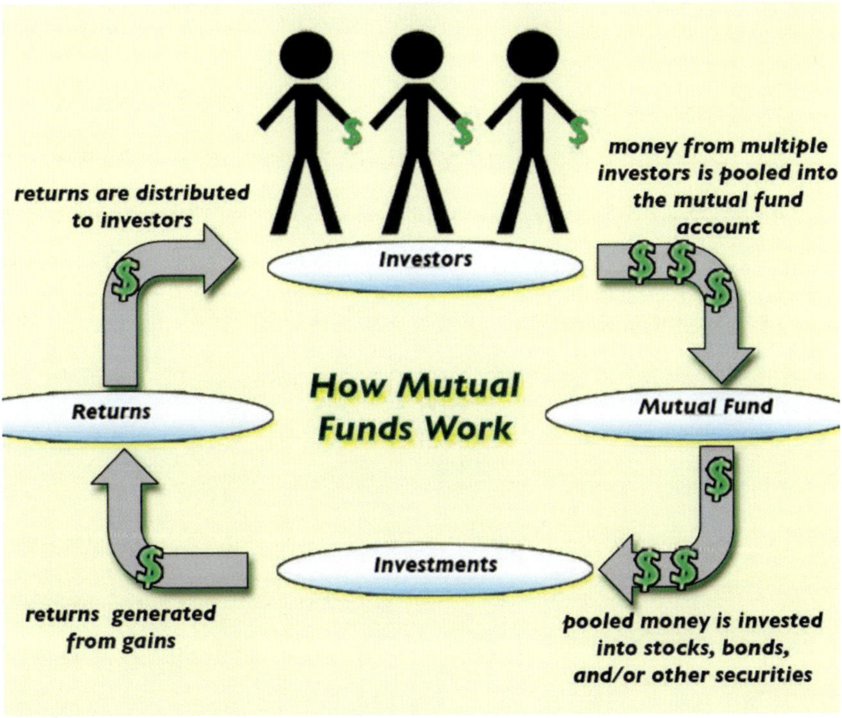

The mutual fund is a simple and elegant concept. The investor who buys shares in a mutual fund effectively hires the fund manager to manage the money. The mutual fund management pools the contributions of as many investors as it can find and buys stocks and bonds. The individual investors become mutual fund shareholders and have no influence on the investment decisions of the fund managers.

Mutual Funds Have Investing Styles

There are thousands of mutual funds from which investors may choose. Each fund has an established investing style. Roughly speaking, there are "bond funds" and "equity funds" that pledge to purchase predominantly bonds and stocks, respectively. Buying shares in an equity mutual fund, for example, has the immediate advantage of diversification. That is, it's common convention to purchase stocks in "round lots" of 100 shares. An individual investment of $5,000 will give 100 shares of a stock with value of $50 per share. Alternatively, a $5,000 investment in an equity mutual fund will give a proportional share in the fund's portfolio of hundreds of stocks. Mutual funds give instant diversification.

Investing styles of funds vary tremendously in order to suit different investors. Clearly, equity funds tend to be more risky than bond funds since stocks are more risky than bonds. Higher risk means, as we've discussed, higher <u>expected</u> return with greater uncertainty of the <u>actual</u> return. Among equity funds there are those that specialize in high-risk equities (generally smaller and younger companies) and low-risk equities (often large, recession-proof firms and utilities).

There are equity funds that focus on specific industries as well. For example, if you want to own semiconductor technology stocks but don't wish to purchase them individually, there are mutual funds that will buy only equity of semiconductor companies. The market defines funds with such focused strategies as "sector funds". A variant of the sector fund is the "country fund". Investors will find stock and bond mutual funds that invest in specific countries or groups of countries (*e.g.*, Europe, Asia, Latin America).

The notion of sector and country funds applies to bonds as well as stocks. Quite often the industry divides bond funds also into two categories of "high grade" (or "investment grade") and "high yield" (or "speculative grade"). The "high grade" funds purchase only bonds with credit ratings between triple-**A** and triple-**B**. The "high yield" funds focus on bonds with ratings of double-**B** and lower. As the name suggests, "high yield" funds pay a higher yield since investors have higher risk of bond defaults.

Mutual funds are a great resource for investors since they provide wide choice in risks and types of investments in stocks and bonds. There is often either no, or a quite small, minimum investment amount. Funds generally permit investors to sell their shares at any time (good liquidity) and share values appear in newspapers and websites (good price transparency). Mutual funds are certainly acceptable investments.

In fact, chapter 4 ("Moving Money") advised sending money directly to a broker's money market fund as a cash account for subsequent investments. Money market funds are a special form of mutual fund that purchase only safe and very short-term debt obligations. Unlike other mutual funds, these money market funds manage themselves so that the individual share price is $1 and this price will very likely **not** fall below $1 (nor rise above $1). The funds simply pay a variable interest rate. In other words, money market funds act like bank accounts. Though there is no explicit insurance against loss, the nature of the money market fund assets reduces the probability of loss to a reasonably low level.

Advantages of Mutual Funds

An advantage of mutual funds is the professional management of your money. A strongly related disadvantage is the fee you pay for this management. Review the fees, purchase commissions and sales charges of each potential mutual fund investment and compare various funds to find those with lowest cost. The cost of management is and should be a key factor in choosing a mutual fund.

It may seem odd that we assign such importance to management fees. For example, if one fund takes 1% of your investment every year and another takes 2%, isn't it possible that the more expensive fund will have better performance? Why not pay for better managers? Recall, though, our extensive discussion of "efficient markets" (chapter 7). While all experts have opinions on which stocks and bonds to buy, nobody consistently beats the market. In other words, you really could do just as well as the fund managers in selecting investments. You're really paying the managers for the instant diversification as well as for the convenience of not having to choose stocks and bonds to buy. So don't pay for "better" managers.

Mutual funds known as "index funds" explicitly acknowledge a manager's inability to beat the market. The manager of an index fund simply purchases the bonds or stocks that match a specific market index (the most well known of which are the S&P 500 and the Dow Jones Industrial Average for stocks). Index fund fees are the lowest of all mutual funds because there's almost no work or thought involved. Such index funds clearly state that their goal is to match the performance of the index. They work! Index funds will reliably give you the performance of the index minus fees as low as 0.2% per year.

Mutual funds tout their track records by showing investment returns for the past few years along with a comparable index return. Almost all such advertisements show that funds apparently do beat the market averages. Let's call this phenomenon "selection deception". Many funds under-perform the market averages, but they don't advertise that fact! Out of 100 funds, 50 may over-perform while 50 under-perform. The 50 over-performers will advertise their returns while the others will not. Though it may make great marketing, the legend of the star fund manager is entirely mythical.

Still, it's useful to see that a fund does have a track record. It likely means the fund has been operating for a few years with the style they advocate. Even though efficient market theory implies that all fund managers are roughly similar, it's best to place your money in established funds with reputable fund management companies.

Disadvantage of Mutual Funds

The primary disadvantage of mutual funds is that they take all, or at least a good part of, the fun out of investing! As we discussed previously, the true fun and meaning of investing is becoming a part of the economy. When you buy IBM stock, for example, you risk your own money and embrace IBM's corporate mission statement as your own. You, personally, help bring computing hardware and software to the world. While this sentiment may seem exaggerated, it's really not. You'll feel it more and more as you continue to invest. This sense of participation will drive you to increase your savings and investment. Purchasing shares of a mutual fund does not give the same <u>feeling</u> of participation although, in strictly economic terms, the participation in the economy remains.

Clearly this is a highly personal distinction. You may feel perfectly content in saving money, sending it to mutual funds, and having your hired managers invest in whatever they deem appropriate. There's absolutely nothing wrong with this practice. But you'll be missing what many people consider to be the "joy of investing". This joy is not just for capitalists! Ironically, it's not uncommon for neo-socialist people and groups to buy stock in specific companies with the goal of raising issues (such as opposition to defense contracting, unequal salaries, and free trade) to all shareholders. When you buy stocks (or bonds) directly, you are a true owner (or lender).

A less important disadvantage specific to bond funds is that the bond fund risk profile differs markedly from that for a single bond. Equity funds, by contrast, simply give diversified equity risk. With a single bond, though, the investor "buys a risk profile" that returns all principal and interest with very high probability at a fixed point in time (the maturity date). With very low probability, the bond will default and give the investor only fifty percent or so of his/her investment. This risk profile is simple and distinctive.

Bond mutual funds, however, have risk profiles much like very-low-risk equity funds. A bond fund has no maturity date on which you'll likely get full principal repayment. Fortunately, there's also no true prospect of a huge 50% loss due to the diversification of owning a share of many bonds. Further, the value of the fund will rise and fall daily due to interest rate and economic news. A bond fund is an investment that rises if the economy does well and interest rates don't rise and falls if the economy is weak and interest rates don't fall. Thus, it differs in several respects from a single bond or small number of bonds of the same maturity. This observation does not disqualify bond funds as investments. Rather, you as the investor must be comfortable with the distinction between individual bonds and bond mutual funds.

11

EXOTIC, UNACCEPTABLE INVESTMENTS

We've discussed stocks, bonds, and mutual funds in preceding chapters and their suitability as "acceptable investments". As a general summary, these instruments are acceptable when they are consistent with your risk tolerance, have good liquidity and price transparency, and satisfy other criteria of chapter 6 ("Acceptable Investments").

But there are many, many more financial instruments other than stocks, bonds, and mutual funds. You may hear friends or commentators recommending investments in currencies, commodities, partnerships, hedge funds, and so on. Futures and options appear to be exciting (and, therefore, better?) alternatives to old-fashioned stocks and bonds. We describe several of these alternatives in this chapter and discuss why virtually all of them are unacceptable for one reason or another. First we distinguish between investing and other activities.

Gambling, Speculating, Hedging, and Investing

A primary argument of this book is that stocks and bonds are the best investments when they suit your risk tolerance. Clearly, we buy such instruments in the hope and expectation that they will pay us more than risk-free investments. Even though we have this hope of gain, there is also the risk of loss. It's reasonable to ask, then, how investing differs from gambling. Dismissive critics, in fact, often refer to the stock market as "a casino".

First let's discuss "speculation". Speculation, as in buying stock today with the plan of selling tomorrow at a higher price, is high-brow gambling. A typical gamble, whether it be purchasing a lottery ticket or playing blackjack or bingo, entails winning or losing money due largely to chance events over which you have no control. Certainly, then, speculating on the value of a company's stock from one day to the next is a form of gambling.

In defense of speculators, one should consider financial market speculation to be *smart* gambling. Depending on the precise trade or position that a speculator takes, he/she will make money, or at least break even, on average. Over the course of many speculative trades, the speculator should have as many winners as losers. The typical Las Vegas gambler is a loser. Further, speculators are good for financial markets. They may be gamblers, but their trading creates market efficiency that benefits everyone.

There's a tremendous difference between investing and speculating. Paradoxically, the explanation of this difference may appear flimsy since it depends as much on the investor's intent as on his/her actions. First, investors take long-term positions (*e.g.*, "buy and hold"). There's much more certainty that a financial asset will increase in value over a long time period than there is of this asset increasing over a short period (such as a week or month). More importantly, we define "investment" as a financial activity that serves a true economic purpose. Companies need owners and lenders. Thus, individual long-term purchases of stocks and bonds benefit both the specific companies and the entire economy.

Like a gambler, the investor takes the risk that the stock or bond market return is uncertain. The investor's actions have broad and constructive economic impact. There's nothing inherently "wrong" with speculation. Our strong advice, though, is to leave speculation to professionals.

In addition to speculating, gambling, and investing is the activity of "hedging". A hedge is a transaction that, by itself, is speculative but serves to reduce an investor's overall risk. For example, an investor may own a specific stock that he/she does not wish to sell. If the investor sells a call option on this stock, which we explain later in this chapter, then the investor's total risk to this stock will fall. The call option itself is speculative but acts as a "hedge" (risk reducer) for this investor who already owns the stock.

Individual investors need concern themselves only with acceptable investments. Speculative and hedging positions are, at best, more complicated than necessary. Quite often these are unacceptable for other reasons as well.

Short Positions

When a speculator believes a stock price will rise, he/she may buy the stock with the intent to sell in the near future at a profit. It's quite possible the stock will not rise as the speculator hopes, but buying the stock does make sense given the speculator's opinion of the stock. The trader's motto is "buy low and sell high".

Now imagine the opposite. A speculator believes a stock is likely to fall. If he/she currently owns the stock, then this speculator would certainly sell. The technique known as "short selling" allows the speculator to sell stock that he/she doesn't own! It's not intuitive but it makes sense (after a great deal of thought). That is, suppose <u>you</u> own IBM stock as a long-term investor. You have no desire to sell. A speculator, on the other hand, believes IBM will fall in value soon. This person asks to borrow your IBM stock and pays you a fee. After you lend your stock to the speculator, he/she sells the stock. If IBM stock does, indeed, fall in value, the speculator will buy it back at the lower price and re-pay the "stock loan" to you by returning the number of shares he/she had borrowed. The short seller's motto is "sell high and buy low"!

When you own a stock or bond, financial people say you are "long" the asset. When you've sold a stock or bond short, then you're "short" the asset. When you're long, you benefit when the asset price rises and lose if the price falls. Similarly, when you're short, you lose if the price rises and win when it falls. Thus, a speculator in a long position is betting that the price will rise while a speculator who is short bets that the price will fall.

Everybody loves to hate short sellers. They're like vultures. But just as vultures perform a critical role for the environment, so do short sellers serve an important function for the financial markets. In addition to adding liquidity to the market, they push the stock price down with their opinions and information. Since the stock price in an efficient market is a consensus of views of all market participants, it's imperative to keep markets open to short sellers. Many politicians and other talking-heads don't get this point. It is not at all "better" for the economy for a speculator to buy (*i.e.*, bet on rising prices) than to sell (*i.e.*, bet on falling prices).

While short sellers are critical for the health of the market, you shouldn't be one of them. Selling short is speculation rather than investing. Short sellers are neither owners nor lenders. They're more like "game players" that inadvertently help the markets and the rest of us. Be polite to them but don't join them.

Futures Contracts

Perhaps as part of a joke, you may have heard of "pork belly futures" contracts. They really exist and they do serve a practical need. Still, you never quite get used to them. There are futures contracts (or just "futures") for many commodities other than pork bellies. The list includes wheat, corn, coffee, oil, natural gas, and major currencies.

All futures contracts have the same general structure. You make an agreement to buy or sell the underlying commodity at a fixed future time at the existing futures price. For example, imagine you "go long" the June 2014 oil futures contract at $100 per barrel. By executing the contract, you agree to pay $100,000 in June 2014 to take delivery of 1,000 barrels of oil. You sign this contract even though you have absolutely no interest in having delivery people stuff 1,000 barrels into your crowded garage. Rather, you hope that the oil price will rise after you enter the contract so that you can "close out" the contract with a profit. Specifically, if the contract price increases to $102 the following day, you can close out your contract and receive $2,000.

In fact, whether you close out or not, the contract will "settle" every day. That is, you'll receive your profit payment daily or, if your position loses, you must make a payment daily. To ensure that you will make any payments when due, you will post a security deposit ("collateral") for all futures contracts. The amount of this collateral is far less than the $100,000 contract size.

Futures contracts are more complex and dangerous than simple purchases of stocks and bonds. In this oil futures trade, the collateral you provide may be only $5,000. With this small "investment", you take full risk to $100,000 worth of oil. Many novice futures investors don't understand this point. They believe the $5,000 is the investment. It's possible your broker will call in less than a week to say you've lost a few thousand dollars and you must send more money to keep the contract open! This aspect of being able to "control" a large investment with a small cash payment (the collateral) is leverage in disguise. Futures contracts are highly leveraged even though you don't explicitly borrow money as with conventional leverage.

Futures contracts generally have high liquidity and price transparency and futures markets tend to be efficient. These contracts do not make acceptable investments for individual investors, however, since they are highly leveraged. Futures positions are not true investments in any case since they are short-term and do not serve economic purposes such as ownership or lending.

Futures are primarily the domain of speculators and hedgers. The speculator will simply have a view that oil prices will rise or fall and will take the appropriate ("long" or "short") position in an oil futures contract. A hedger would be a company, like an airline or power generation plant, that expects to buy oil-related products in June 2013. This company would enter a long oil futures position now to "lock in" a future price of oil. That is, if oil prices rise, the company makes money in the futures contract while losing money in the higher purchase cost for oil in June. There are natural hedgers on both sides of all futures contracts. There are also speculators. The market needs both groups.

You may encounter an advisor who will tell you that executing futures contracts or investing in funds that execute futures contracts is advantageous because it diversifies your investment portfolio. For example, if you have an equity portfolio, then taking positions on oil, currencies, pork bellies, or whatever with futures contracts will diversify your risk. If the stock market falls, these other commodities are unlikely to fall simultaneously. There's some wisdom in this advice, but we reject it nonetheless. If you'd like exposure to oil, currencies, gold, *et cetera*, then it's better to buy stocks and bonds with the desired risk. That is, buy stock of oil and gold mining companies. Or buy bonds in foreign currencies if you want the currency risk. Such purchases will be true and acceptable investments and will give the diversification you seek.

Options

Many companies give their executives "stock options" as part of their total compensation. Executives who own such options have the right to buy their company's stock at a fixed price (the "strike price") until a fixed time in the future (the "expiration date"). These options are valuable precisely because the executives have the option of whether or not to "exercise" (*i.e.*, buy the stock at the strike price). For example, imagine the stock price is now $36 per share and the executive has the option to buy 10,000 shares at $40 per share with expiration date in one year. The executive would not exercise now to buy the 10,000 shares because she'd pay $40 per share when she'd be able to pay just $36 in the market. But, if the strike price is $30 rather than $40, then the executive can use the options to earn an immediate profit. She may buy the 10,000 shares for $30 per share ($300,000) and then sell to the market at $36 per share ($360,000).

Let's step back. Executive stock options are a very, very small segment of the option world. Investors buy and sell options in the market. It's rare to have an employer or anybody else simply *give* you options. (Advice: Take them if this happens to you.) When you buy an option, the worst possible outcome is that the expiration date will come and you will never have been able to realize a profit by exercising the option. So, your investment may fall to zero with fairly high probability. Unlike futures contracts, though, there is no requirement to make more payments. The best possible outcome, on the other hand, is that you will be able to exercise your option and you may earn much more than the original option cost. Options, therefore, generally have very high risk and very high potential return.

Options can give the investor either the right to buy or the right to sell. Our executive stock option example conferred the right to buy the company's stock. The market defines the right to buy as a "call option". The right to sell, conversely, is a "put option". As a side comment, companies sometimes issue "warrants" during a merger or acquisition. A warrant is simply a call option on the stock of the issuing company.

If an investor believes a stock will increase in value, he/she may either buy the stock or buy a call option on the stock. To compare these two possibilities, let's consider the earlier example of the option to buy a company's stock at $40 per share with expiration date in one year in which the stock price is now $36. A typical cost (or "premium") for this call option might be $3 per share. An investor who buys the stock at $36 will earn $4 or $14 per share, respectively, if the stock price after one year rises to $40 or $50. The call option investor, on the other hand, pays the $3 premium and will have either a worthless option (1-year stock price at $40) or an option with value of $10 (1-year stock price of $50). While the stock investor gains either 11% or 39% in the two scenarios, the option investor loses everything or more than triples the investment (*i.e.*, gives more than 200% return)! Purchases of call options require much less money than buying the underlying stock, give a far greater probability of total loss, and also give far greater potential reward relative to the initial cash invested.

An investor who believes a stock will fall in value may either sell the stock short or buy a put option on the stock. The put option gives the right to sell the stock at a pre-defined strike price. Imagine the investor buys a put option to sell 10,000 shares of a $36 stock at the strike price of $30. If the stock falls to $25, the put option investor would buy the shares at $25 and then exercise the put option so that he/she can sell these same shares at $30. That sequence gives an immediate $5 per share ($50,000) gain.

In addition to options on many stocks, there are options on Treasury bonds, futures contracts, and various market indices such as the S&P 500. Many of these markets are moderately liquid and there is good price transparency. We do <u>not</u>, however, consider options to be acceptable investments for individual investors. They are short-term and they constitute neither ownership nor lending. That is, they do not serve a true economic purpose. Speculators and hedgers are the most natural participants in option markets.

We should add that it is possible for individuals to use options in a low-risk manner by hedging existing positions. For example, if you own 1,000 shares of IBM stock, you may buy put options on 1,000 or fewer IBM shares. The put options protect you against a fall in value of the IBM stock you own. In this case, buying the put options is akin to buying insurance. Alternatively or additionally, you may sell call options on some or all of your IBM shares. Here you receive a premium with the risk that the option contract may force you to sell your shares at a strike price that will be less than the future market price. Both of these option strategies carry little risk since you already own the underlying IBM shares.

After all this discussion, though, there's no compelling reason for individual investors to jump into options. Placing options in your portfolio adds needless complication. You will not outperform the strategy of buying and holding stocks and bonds.

Hedge Funds

Hedge funds are to mutual funds as a Lamborghini is to a

Ford Taurus. The differences are more important than the similarities. Like mutual funds, hedge funds solicit investments from individuals. These individuals effectively pay the fund managers to invest their money.

Securities and Exchange Commission (SEC) regulations for mutual funds do not apply to hedge funds. As a trade-off for lighter regulation, hedge funds may not solicit investors through public advertisements and must accept only wealthy investors. Typical minimum investments are greater than $1 million. The purpose of restrictions on advertising and investor wealth is to ensure that only "sophisticated" investors will throw their money into hedge funds.

The first ramification of the absence of regulation is that hedge funds do not disclose their investing strategy. You won't know what your fund is buying! Generally, hedge fund strategy is to take on a financial risk of some sort with equities, bonds, or "derivative" contracts and then add related trades that neutralize this risk. If the fund can find this "hedge" trade that still leaves some profit, then the fund will earn profit with no, or very little, risk. This concept is the origin of the "hedge fund" name. If such opportunities, in which two offsetting trades give reasonable profit and very little risk, truly exist, then the fund will guard these trades in secrecy. If others learn of this two-trade strategy, they will execute the same trades and drive prices in a manner that eliminates the profit.

Even when a trade and its hedge give "reasonable" profit, the profit is small compared to simple bond yields. Hence, the hedge fund strategy makes sense only if the fund leverages itself significantly by, for example, borrowing at least ten times as much money as investors have contributed. Finally, consider that perfectly efficient markets do not have such "arbitrage" opportunities (see chapter 7 on Efficient Markets) in which a pair of trades gives profit with zero risk. Thus, hedge funds must typically invest in inefficient markets (such as seldom-traded bonds or in minor currencies) with moderate to poor liquidity.

Hedge fund investors pay fees that are typically much higher than those of mutual funds on the theory that their fund managers are brilliant, swashbuckling pirates rampaging the financial market seas. Investors should not pay the fees. The premise of hedge funds is that, including all fees, "smart people" will consistently outperform simpler investments you would make for yourself. There's no proof that any hedge fund manager can make this claim. Hedge funds merely have a mystique that captivates some investors.

For several reasons, hedge funds are not "acceptable investments" for individual investors. First, they are often illiquid. You must generally "commit" your investment for a fixed period of time. Second, there is little price transparency. That is, it's not clear how much your investment is worth at any time. Finally, why throw your money into the "black box" secrecy of a hedge fund? For all you know, the fund may have a huge long position in European pomegranates and a matching short interest in Asian kumquats. Investing is more than a game to make money. True investors want to know how and why they're participating in the world economy.

Though individuals should shun hedge funds, the funds do serve a valuable purpose for financial markets. Markets always benefit from greater participation. Hedge funds add liquidity for everybody. Also, institutions may find hedge funds to be useful investments due to the diversification argument. For example, an insurance company with a bond portfolio may seek an investment that is not correlated to the bond portfolio return. That is, if the bonds fall in value the hedge fund investment is likely to perform better than the bonds. We add the appendix "Hedge Funds in More Depth" at the conclusion of this book to bolster this discussion for readers with good knowledge of the financial markets.

Initial Public Offerings

Many companies are "private" in the sense that they have not sold common stock to the public. There may be one owner or a small group of owners that wishes to sell all or, more likely, a portion of the company to the public. This first sale of stock to the public is the "initial public offering" (IPO). IPOs are exciting and often attract tremendous publicity. Looking only at the heyday of Internet stocks of the late 1990's, it appears that IPO stock prices invariably skyrocket.

Our advice for IPOs is simple: avoid them. The risk profile of common stock is not troublesome for investors with equity risk appetite. Rather, it's the price of the stock that renders IPO investments unacceptable. When companies issue stock for the first time, they really don't know what price to ask of investors. Regulatory issues encourage companies to sell stock at a low price relative to the company's best estimate. The good news, then, is that IPOs are often a great opportunity. The bad news is that such great opportunities rarely come to individual investors. If an advisor or broker does call with an IPO investment for you, it's most likely for a hot dog rotisserie manufacturer or something similar. Very simply, don't buy into IPOs since an efficient market has not set the price.

In May 2012, Facebook provided the most spectacular and infamous IPO of recent memory. The company and its investment banks succeeded in selling more than 400 million shares to the public at $38 per share. Over the ensuing three months the share price fell below $20. While Facebook and its bankers may have believed the traded price would remain near or above the $38 launch, the market's verdict was that true "fair value" was far lower. Like all pre-IPO stocks, Facebook did not have a market-vetted share price prior to the share issuance.

Partnerships

Partnerships resemble mutual funds to some extent in that you join with other investors to pool money for asset purchases. Instead of stocks and bonds, the assets tend to be real estate or specialized equipment (*e.g.*, oil drilling, construction equipment, *et cetera*). Unlike mutual funds, you become a "limited partner" rather than a shareowner in the venture. Advisors tout tax benefits since the issuers deliberately construct partnerships to take advantage of odd tax rules. For example, you may be able to deduct depreciation on oil drilling equipment from your federal taxes.

Partnerships are bad news. Forget them. They immediately fail the tests of liquidity and price transparency. You may never get out of them before maturity or you'll never know the fair value of your partnership interest. As a rule, de-emphasize the tax considerations of investing. You're "taking your eye off the ball" when you dwell on tax consequences. (See chapter 14 on Tax Considerations.)

Ponzi Schemes

It is something of a joke that we include "Ponzi schemes" as exotic and unacceptable investments. Ponzi schemes are fraudulent so they are, of course, unacceptable. But there are lessons to consider at the intersection of human nature and money.

Charles Ponzi offered "investments" to the public beginning in January 1920 that purported to return as much as 100% within 90 days. Investors enthusiastically chipped in several million dollars within the first months. The offering was a fraud because Ponzi had no workable investment strategy. That is, he did not invest the funds he received at a rate that would permit him to legitimately pay his clients such huge returns. Ponzi simply spent money on himself and stashed the remainder in his own bank account. Authorities, the press, and the public uncovered the deception in August of the same year. Everybody took losses and Ponzi went to jail.

But why did it work even for just a few months? Why would any "normal person" invest any significant amount? Imagine yourself in the situation of "testing" the investment with a small amount such as $50. At the maturity date, you go to the teller window and receive $100 – which is your earlier investment plus the promised return. What do you do now with your $100? Our brains would not even need to do a calculation! There must be some deeper, reflexive, non-analytical region in the brain that would take charge and hand that $100 straight back to the agent (to "invest" for another period).

The generic "Ponzi scheme", then, invokes the false promise of good investment return to solicit money that the investment provider simply steals or uses to repay others. Temporary success of the fraudulent Ponzi scheme relies on most investors keeping their money in the deal and on an increasing flow of money from new investors that will be available to pay the old investors who do choose to cash out. Ponzi schemes always fail eventually – they must fail. At some point the desire of existing investors to take money out of the deal will exceed the inflow of new money. Any rumor of the scheme's inability to pay produces dramatic failure as many investors demand to be repaid immediately.

The champion of all Ponzi schemes is the discovery of Bernie Madoff in December 2008. All told, Madoff's investors claimed his liability to them was $65 billion. In a perverse sense, Madoff can claim the success of the largest and likely the longest running fraud of this type in history. Several factors explain this "success". First, the return to the investors was only about 12% per annum. Madoff did not need to promise a large return that would make the scheme burn out more quickly. Rather, this return was very steady month after month and year after year. The low volatility of the return made it attractive.

Second, Madoff was well known in the financial world with a solid reputation. From all appearances, he should not have needed to earn his living illegally. Those who may have suspected Madoff years before 2008 likely concluded it was irrational to think he would steal money. What we remember only in hindsight is that crime is not rational. Mental illness, which some suspect is part of the story, is not rational.

Ponzi schemes are everywhere. Due to the simplicity of the fraud and the chord it strikes in human nature, our guess is that this type of deception has existed for centuries past and will persist well into the future. There are many Ponzi schemes worldwide that have not yet been detected. One reason we have such sweeping confidence in the durability of this fraud is that they even happen by accident! Consider an investment manager who starts out with an honest business model. He/she takes clients' money and buys real assets in the hope and expectation that the assets will perform well and both clients and manager will profit. But imagine then that the assets perform poorly. What does the manager do? The honest and most likely manager action is to inform all clients of the losses stemming from poor asset performance. Some managers in some circumstances, though, will not be honest. The dishonest manager may choose not to report actual returns in the hope that the same assets (or other assets) will perform better later so that the manager can "win back" the lost money. When the manager cannot recoup the losses, the activity takes on the appearance of a Ponzi scheme.

Sound far-fetched? Not at all! This is how many scandals play out in the financial world. It's a Shakespearean dilemma. The manager has knowledge (asset losses) that will be harmful to disclose to others. The normal human reaction is "don't disclose it!" While the great majority (?) of professionals have sufficient integrity to overcome this human weakness, there are plenty of cases in which "integrity" loses the battle.

The point of this discussion is that you need to avoid Ponzi schemes and all other frauds. Guidelines to steer clear of such horrendous problems are: (i) follow the recommendations of Acceptable Investments (chapters 6 and 11); (ii) if you do choose to stray from the advice of chapters 6 and 11, then be sure there is a well known, independent auditor responsible for overseeing any fund or activity in which you invest and be sure to read the auditor's reports; (iii) avoid any investment that "promises" a return without acknowledging that there is risk of loss; and (iv) do not invest more than, say, 20% of your funds in any one vehicle.

(a)

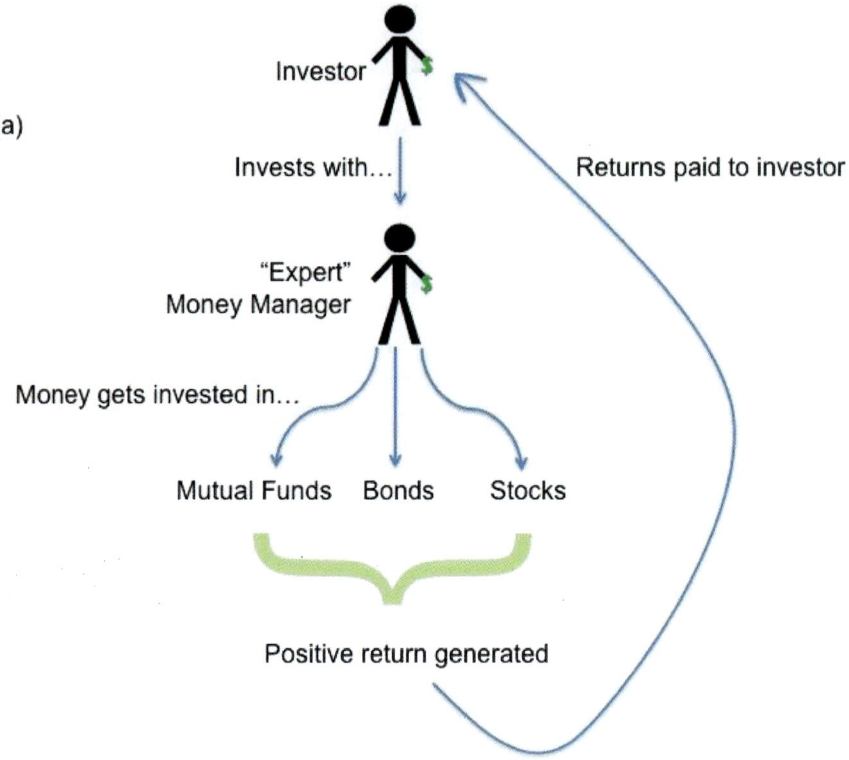
Investor
Invests with…
Returns paid to investor
"Expert"
Money Manager
Money gets invested in…
Mutual Funds
Bonds
Stocks
Positive return generated

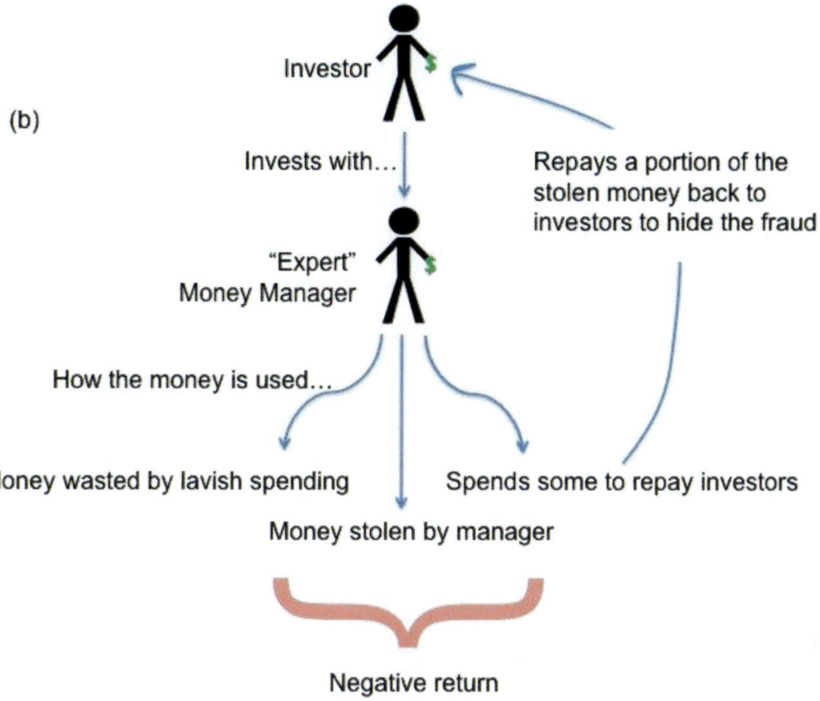

Ponzi Scheme: **(a) Shows the flow of money that the investor assumes. (b) Shows a more accurate movement of money invested in a Ponzi scheme fraud.**

12

FINANCIAL ADVISORS

Earlier chapters mentioned the importance of financial advisors. We emphasize and expand on this subject here, but we refer you as well to the structured discussion of this topic of the Certified Financial Planner Board of Standards, Inc. at http://www.cfp.net/learn/knowledgebase.asp?id=6.

As general advice, we consider it best that you manage your own money and serve as your own financial advisor. As enunciated in this book, we believe the important underlying principles are sufficiently simple that you can gain comfort and confidence in saving and investing your own money. The time and effort you spend managing your own finances is certainly a cost, but one clear benefit is that you are "in charge" and completely aware of your financial position.

As with any "general advice", it may not apply in your specific situation. Hence, if you do decide to engage an advisor, we provide thoughts on choosing and working with this advisor. The most important element is that you must be comfortable with the advisor and have confidence in him/her. If this relationship chemistry is absent or, even worse, negative, then don't go forward with the advisor. There's no reason to mix your money with a weak or bad relationship.

One reason to emphasize "relationship" is that a competent advisor must get very personal with you. He/she will want to know all your financial details (assets, debts, current income, likely future income and expenses, how long you plan to continue working, *et cetera*) and personal information (ages and health of you and family members, expectations of who you will need to support in the future or who might support you, *et cetera*). Clearly this is one incentive to be your own advisor! Nobody can enjoy sharing so much information with an outsider.

The advisor needs all these financial and personal aspects of your life to prepare prudent spending and investing recommendations. Further, through direct discussion, he/she must learn your personal risk tolerance as described earlier in chapter 5. If you begin working with an advisor and he/she does not seek in-depth personal and financial information of this sort before proposing investments, then you should terminate the advisor.

Bear in mind that the financial advisor cannot and should not guarantee or imply that he/she will "beat the market" or "outperform other advisors" investing your money. The advisor's job is to recommend and explain to you investments that fit your risk tolerance, time horizon, and other specific needs. The recommended investments should conform to our guidelines for "acceptable investments" in chapter 6. Based on the concept of market efficiency of chapter 7, your advisor should not claim the ability to "beat the market".

Even with a financial advisor, remain as involved and knowledgeable in the spending and investment decision as possible. Expect and insist that the advisor explain investment proposals, for example. If you don't understand or are not comfortable with a recommendation, then ask questions until you reach the point at which you can say "yes" or "no". Do not hesitate to decline an advisor's investment idea for any reason or even no reason. It's your money!

Maxwell
Consulting

13

HOME MORTGAGES

In chapter 6 we made the point in passing that houses are not suitable investments. Houses are not liquid – that is, selling a house requires work, fees, and time. When you do sell your house, there is little clarity on the price you'll receive until the sale is agreed. As investments, therefore, houses violate our principles of liquidity and price transparency.

Though houses are poor investments, go ahead and buy a house! You and your family need a place to live and you may prefer the advantages of ownership over renting an apartment or house. Just do not think of your house as one of your investments. Further, we consider the purchase of a house to be the only occasion for which borrowing is acceptable for those of us who are not financial professionals. As we stated earlier, we advise against maintaining a credit card balance (a form of borrowing) or taking out car loans, student loans, boat loans, *et cetera*.

There's a debate that pops up every once in a while with the question "is a house an asset or a liability?" Though not an investment, your house is an asset. The higher the value of this asset, the better it is for your net worth. When you borrow money to buy the house, the borrowing is a liability. Clearly, the lower the balance of your borrowing, the better it is for your net worth.

How Mortgages Work

The borrowing transaction for a house is the mortgage. Here's how mortgages work. Let's say you've agreed to pay $200,000 for a house and you have $50,000 in savings for this purchase. Additional charges known as "closing costs" and mortgage taxes add $5,000 - $10,000. Let's choose $10,000 for the sake of this example. That means you need $210,000 to buy the house.

Thus, you need to borrow $160,000 (the $210,000 for the house and additional costs minus the $50,000 you already have). You find a bank willing to lend the $160,000. You, the seller of the house, and various lawyers meet at the bank. After exchanging and signing many documents and checks, the net result is that you and the bank have paid $200,000 to the seller, you have paid the closing costs and taxes, the seller has transferred title of the house to you, and the bank gains a lien on your house for the ultimate payment of the mortgage. (As a friend of ours has joked, if you have any money left at the end of this bank meeting, then somebody has made a mistake.)

This last point regarding the lien is critically important. The bank does not own your house. You own the house. The lien gives the bank the right to seize the house and sell it if you fail to make the mortgage payments. Think about it - $160,000 is a lot of money! The bank would not lend you this much money without the house as collateral. A loan without collateral is "unsecured" while a loan with collateral is "secured". Credit card and college tuition loans are unsecured. Auto loans and mortgages are secured by the car and house, respectively.

Mortgage Details

You make mortgage payments every month until the stated maturity date which is typically 30 years in the future. In a fixed-rate mortgage (FRM), you pay the same interest rate for the life of the loan. Using 4% per annum as the mortgage rate in our example, the first monthly <u>interest</u> payment would be 4% x $160,000 x (1/12) = $533. The <u>actual</u> monthly mortgage payment will be higher than this $533 for several reasons. First, you pay principal as well as interest every month. At the end of the mortgage loan, you will have paid the principal (originally $160,000) down to zero.

The actual mortgage payment also includes property taxes due on your house. The bank places the tax portion of the monthly payment into escrow and then pays the taxes on your behalf when they are due. The bank itself does not keep these property taxes. This is not simply a convenience the bank offers. Rather, the bank wants to be sure you pay the taxes! If you fail to pay the taxes, the local government has the right to seize your house. The government's right to take your house and sell it for past-due taxes is superior to the lien the bank has on the house to recoup its mortgage loan.

Some mortgages are "adjustable-rate" rather than "fixed-rate". In an adjustable-rate mortgage (ARM), the interest rate you pay goes up or down in a manner that tracks a specified interest rate index. General wisdom is that FRMs are safer than ARMs for the evident reason that your payment will never go up (other than for increases in property tax rates).

You may deduct interest you pay for "eligible mortgages" – as the Internal Revenue Service (IRS) defines them – from income for your calculation of Federal income tax. Similar deductibility generally exists as well for state income tax determination. To be helpful, your "itemized deductions" with the mortgage interest (and property taxes and other costs) would need to exceed your "standard deduction". You'd also need to choose to itemize deductions in the IRS Form 1040 and complete the associated Schedule A. Thus, with added complexity to your tax filing, you will recoup some of the mortgage interest payment. Reducing the tax liability is welcome. But don't let the relatively small benefit of tax rebate coax you into a larger mortgage.

How the Bank Thinks

When deciding whether to extend a mortgage loan to you, the bank has three primary criteria. They are: your personal credit history; the amount of money you wish to borrow relative to the value of the house; and the size of your projected monthly payment for all debt relative to your income. The general measure for "personal credit history" is your "credit score". Well known credit score providers are FICO (formerly known as "Fair Isaac Corporation"), TransUnion, Experian, and Equifax. Though imprecise, a credit score of 620 has been the rough dividing line between "prime" and "sub-prime" loans. The credit score range is 300 to 850 with higher score indicating higher borrower credit quality.

The ratio of mortgage loan to the value of the house is "loan-to-value" (LTV). Lower LTV is good for the bank. If the bank ever needs to seize your house when you don't pay the mortgage, it is more likely to be able to pay off the loan with the sale proceeds. For example, if your house has a reputed value of $100,000 and the mortgage balance is just $60,000, then the bank is highly likely to be able to sell the house for more than $60,000 after foreclosure.

In this case above, the LTV is 60% ($60,000 / $100,000) because the mortgage loan amount is $60,000 while the reputed house value is $100,000. If we say instead that the loan amount is $90,000, then the LTV would be 90% ($90,000 / $100,000). If the bank were to foreclose on this 90% LTV loan, there is a very good chance it would <u>not</u> be able to sell the house for $90,000 or more. Even though we describe the reputed house value as $100,000, sales at foreclosure or any type of "forced" or "distressed" sale generally result in less than expected prices. Further, in the real estate world nobody truly believes valuations such as the $100,000 of this example. Such numbers are merely "educated guesses" of the appraiser. The only value that matters is what a real buyer is willing to pay and this value is known only at point of sale.

As these examples show, the bank prefers lower LTV in its lending and is more likely to reject loan applications as LTV increases. The benchmark LTV over the past several decades has been 80%. Excluding closing costs and mortgage taxes, that means house buyers need a 20% down payment to gain approval for this "standard mortgage". One of the many reasons for the U.S. mortgage crisis that began in 2007 and continues through 2013 is that many banks and investors approved mortgage loans with LTV greater than 80%. If there is one simple lesson from the Crisis, it is to keep LTV at 80% or below. Non-government lenders appear to have learned this lesson.

Before we move on, let us say that banks do not want to foreclose on houses to retrieve the funds they had lent. The foreclosure process itself is expensive. It is terrible publicity for the bank. No employee of the bank enjoys his/her role in seizing a house from current occupants. But that's the agreement. If laws or judicial foot-dragging compel the bank to permit owners to remain in their houses without paying the mortgage, then the rational response is for the bank to stop new lending.

As a final comment on LTV, there are two additional advantages of loans with low LTV. First, a borrower with low LTV has a correspondingly higher down payment. More precisely, we should say the borrower's equity (house value minus outstanding loan amount) is higher. Borrowers with greater equity are less likely to default on their mortgages. Second, the high down payment of the borrower with a low-LTV loan shows that the borrower is good managing money. He/she demonstrates ability to save money by paying the high down payment. Such borrowers are likely to manage their mortgage payments well. Borrowers with <u>high</u> LTV are weak for corresponding reasons. A borrower with little or no equity (or even negative equity) is far more likely to default than the average borrower since there is "nothing to lose". Further, a borrower who can make a down payment of only, say, 5% or less for the purchase of a house has not demonstrated the ability to manage and save money. What evidence does the lender have that this borrower will muster the additional financial discipline that the monthly mortgage payment will require?

The last of the three primary criteria for bank lending decisions is debt-to-income ratio (DTI). The DTI is the borrower's monthly payment for all debt such as credit cards and auto loans plus the mortgage payment divided by the borrower's gross monthly income. Clearly a DTI of 100% is "impossible" since the borrower would be paying his/her entire income to debt obligations. There would be nothing left to pay income taxes, buy food, *et cetera*. Generally, a DTI of less than 20% is "good". A DTI of 30% or so is "a stretch, but likely okay". DTI of 45% and higher is the mark of a highly risky loan.

How You Should Think

We discussed above the three primary criteria that the bank uses to determine whether to lend to you for the purchase of a house. Don't let the bank make your decision for you. Just because there's a willing lender does not mean the mortgage loan is a good idea for you. Beyond the obvious thought that you want a low interest rate and low closing costs, your analysis is similar in some ways to that of the bank.

High LTV is a risk to the bank, but it's also a risk to you! A mortgage is a long-term commitment on your part. Don't saddle yourself with a higher loan amount and payment obligation than necessary. There are two ways to decrease the initial LTV: save more money for a higher down payment or buy a less expensive house. Do not simply buy the most expensive house that the mortgage amount permits. That's a trap. Do not be a victim of a failed mortgage by borrowing more than you really need. You may have friends or "television advisors" who suggest that high LTV is "good" because, if house values go down or you have personal setbacks, you can stick the bank with the loss by walking away from the mortgage. Our advice is not to manage your finances and commitments with this attitude.

Likewise, keeping your DTI low is in your best interests. Just as with LTV, increasing your down payment or buying a less expensive house will lower the DTI. The higher the DTI the more you diminish financial freedom by having a relatively large required monthly payment that reduces your ability to invest. When computing your DTI, also question whether your house purchase should be based on both incomes if there are two working adults in the family. If you have two incomes, why make both of them "hostage" to the house? Yes, it's nice to have the bigger and more impressive house that two incomes can purchase. But you are sacrificing freedom and security by committing both adults to continue working for income.

Refinancing

U.S. mortgages have an interesting quirk. The borrower is

permitted to pay down the mortgage at any time prior to maturity without penalty. Most loan agreements that are not home mortgages do not have this feature. Thus, a borrower may take out a fixed-rate mortgage for 30 years at an interest rate of 8% per annum. If the prevailing mortgage rate two years later has dropped to 5% per annum, the borrower has the option to "refinance".

In this example, let's say Bank A made the original mortgage loan at 8% per annum. When rates have fallen to 5% per annum, the borrower can apply to Bank B for a new mortgage at this lower rate. (Bank A and Bank B could literally be the same bank. It's easier to separate them for this discussion.) The idea is that the Bank B loan amount will be paid to Bank A to terminate the original mortgage. The borrower's new mortgage with Bank B will have a lower monthly payment due to the lower 5% per annum interest rate.

This outcome is certainly "good" for the borrower and he/she should take reasonable advantage of this refinancing option when it exists. One complication in the analysis is that the borrower will pay closing costs to Bank B and mortgage taxes on the new loan. As a result, the homeowner must increase the size of the mortgage to pay the additional charges or pay them out-of-pocket. Further, with the refinancing, the borrower will extend the maturity of the loan and thereby make payments farther into the future.

Even with these considerations, there will exist circumstances in which refinancing is a good decision. The "calculation" of the advantage is not simple. We consider Dr. Andy Kalotay to be one of the world's experts on this topic. Dr. Kalotay provides a mortgage calculator at the site http://analytics.kalotay.com/refival/analysis.do. This calculation considers the specific characteristics of the existing and new mortgage loans and determines whether the refinancing is "good" or "bad" for the homeowner.

Our refinancing example assumes the mortgage rate has decreased significantly so that the monthly payment will decline after switching to a new mortgage. But many homeowners prior to the 2007 mortgage crisis refinanced their mortgages simply to receive cash. Here's how it worked. Imagine you bought a house for $300,000 and borrowed $240,000 for an initial LTV of 80% ($240,000 / $300,000). Three years go by and the appraised value of your house grows to $400,000. When you approach Bank B for a new mortgage to pay down the original mortgage of Bank A, you ask to borrow $320,000 instead of $240,000 (the latter value being the approximate remaining principal of the Bank A mortgage). Notice that borrowing $320,000 for a $400,000 house value maintains the LTV at 80%. Bank B pays the remaining $80,000 ($320,000 - $240,000) to you in cash! Popular phrases for this activity are "taking money out of your house" and "using your house as an ATM" and "cash-out refinancing".

Our advice is to avoid this second form of refinancing. It merely adds to your total debt. Common explanations are that homeowners can use the cash extracted from the cash-out refinancing to make home improvements or to pay other bills or to pay down other debt. Yes, but we suggest you use "real money" for these purposes. As other chapters discuss, save your money by cutting expenses well below your income. Use this real cash flow both for new investments and for the home improvements, paying bills, and paying down debt.

Stay Focused on the Investments

Companies, governments, and individuals must all manage their debt just as they manage their assets. This chapter described the primary (if not only) debt obligation that individuals should incur. Although refinancing the mortgage is a viable debt management tool, we recommend that individuals focus the greater amount of their attention on saving, investing, managing assets, and in adding value to the world in work and life. Don't focus on the mortgage.

Yet having a mortgage does raise an investment question. When should the homeowner pay down the mortgage early? In refinancing, one borrows from Bank B to pay the mortgage from Bank A. But the borrower also has the option to pay the Bank A mortgage from excess cash or by selling other investments. In fact, this action is easier than refinancing. There's no negotiation with a Bank B. There are no additional charges. Further, paying down a mortgage early can mean paying the entire outstanding balance or paying any smaller amount. For example, if the monthly mortgage payment is $1,000, the borrower might choose to pay $1,100 every month. The bank will reduce the mortgage principal amount by $100 in this case for every payment that has this $100 excess.

Many homeowners have an opinion on this topic, but we've never seen a rigorous solution. Our rule of thumb is that paying down the mortgage early by making voluntarily larger payments is an investment. The investment is "risk-free" and pays you a yield equal to the mortgage interest rate. (While you lose some mortgage interest deduction for tax purposes, this loss is equivalent to the tax you would pay on the interest of a real investment.) The amount of voluntary early payment of the mortgage, then, should be higher when the mortgage rate is higher simply because the higher rate is a better "investment yield" and there is no risk in this investment of paying down the mortgage.

This analysis has one drawback, though. The investment of paying more than the required mortgage payment is illiquid. Once you make that additional payment, you cannot call the bank the following month and ask for the money back. Stated differently, you cannot sell this (fictitious) investment. Since liquidity is one of our chapter 6 "principles of acceptable investments", we do not consider this early payment of the mortgage to be a "true" investment.

To accommodate the "illiquidity disadvantage" of paying down the mortgage, we recommend simply that you use your best judgment. Pay down your mortgage earlier than required only to the extent you will have ample liquidity (*i.e.*, cash held within your bank and investment accounts) remaining and only when the mortgage rate is significantly higher than the market risk-free interest rate. As a reminder, there will also be occasions in which refinancing the entire mortgage at a lower prevailing interest rate will be the better alternative.

As a superb reference to deeper discussion of this and many other mortgage topics, we refer interested readers to "A Financial Analysis of Consumer Mortgage Decisions" by Andy Kalotay and Qi Fu, copyright *Research Institute for Housing America*, June 2009, available at http://www.mbaa.org/files/Research/AFinancialAnalysisofConsumerMortgageDecisions.pdf .

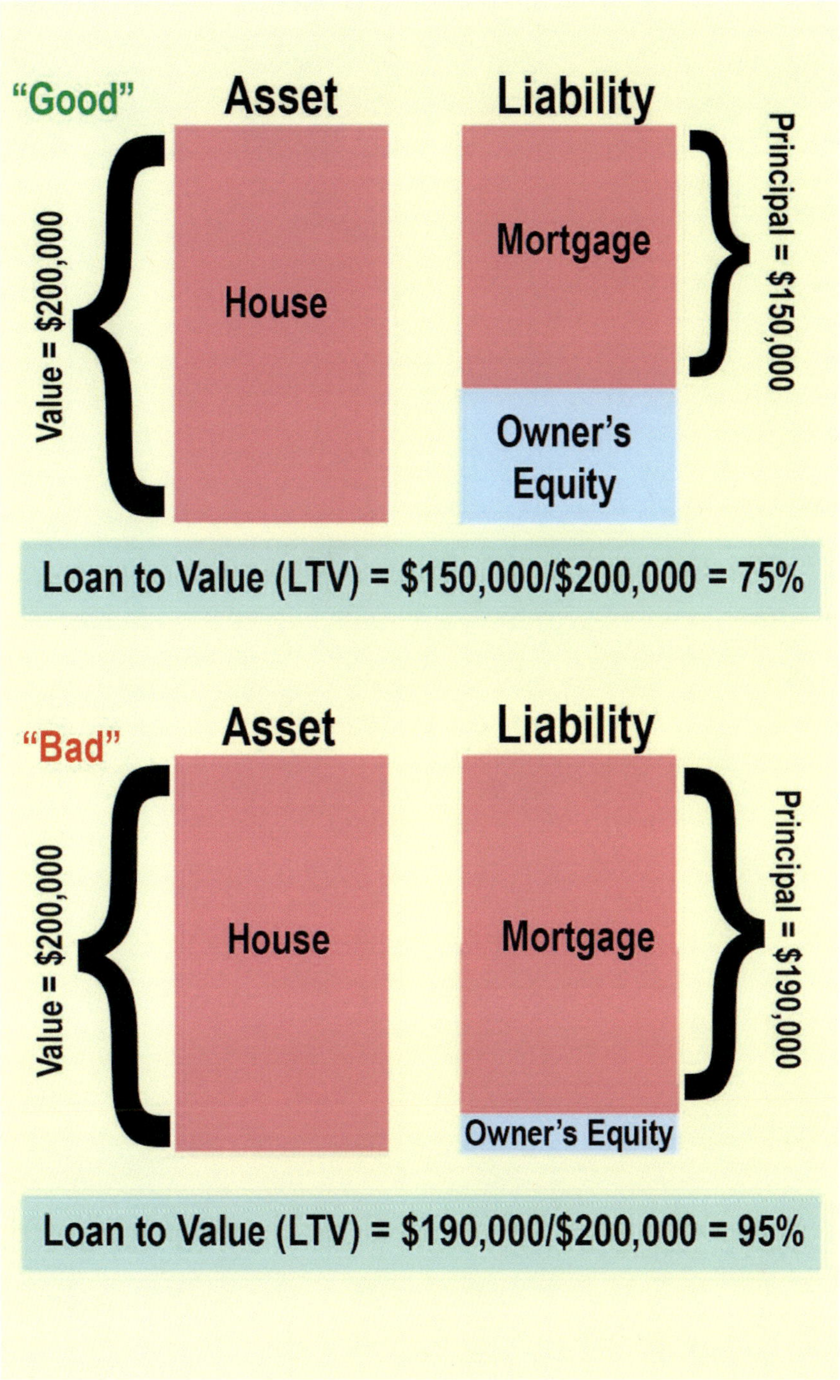
"Good"
Asset
Liability
Value = $200,000
House
Mortgage
Owner's Equity
Principal = $150,000
Loan to Value (LTV) = $150,000/$200,000 = 75%
"Bad"
Asset
Liability
Value = $200,000
House
Mortgage
Owner's Equity
Principal = $190,000
Loan to Value (LTV) = $190,000/$200,000 = 95%

14

TAX CONSIDERATIONS

Death and taxes: if you have a choice, go for the taxes. That doesn't mean you have to like the taxes, though.

Investment Tax Treatment

In addition to the tax you pay on your income, you will pay taxes on your investment gains. Your investment income adds to your employment income so that the higher, total income puts you in a higher tax bracket. Yet different investments have different tax treatments. Interest payments from bonds (and from bond mutual funds) give tax liability as if they were "ordinary income". A capital gain, which is the profit of buying a stock or bond and selling later at a higher price, has preferred tax treatment. If you owned the bond for more than a year, the Federal tax rate (typically 15% or 20%) is lower than that for "ordinary income". For ownership of one year or less, there is no distinction between the capital gain tax rate and that for "ordinary income".

Similarly, US Federal tax laws give the lower rate (15% or 20% for the higher income categories) for dividend income if the investor has owned the stock for more than sixty days during the dividend period. Hence, the tax system currently encourages long-term ownership.

It is certainly possible to experience a capital loss rather than a gain upon selling your stock or bond at a lower price than you paid. Losses become deductions from taxable income just as gains are increases to income. The tax code limits net capital losses in any tax year to $3,000 for individuals. We can only guess this is the government's way to encourage investors not to lose money. Taxpayers may carry capital losses in excess of $3,000 into their tax returns for future years.

When you own individual stocks and bonds, you realize capital gains or losses when you sell the stocks and bonds. The gains and losses increase or decrease the taxable income of the year in which you sell. You may have owned the investment for ten years, but the capital gain or loss affects only the taxes of the year of sale unless you need to carry losses forward. As we discussed in the buy-and-hold strategy of chapter 8 on "Stocks", you should ideally hold your equity investments "forever". In practice, this means you sell your stocks during retirement years as necessary. Since your total income falls in retirement, the tax you pay on selling your stock will be less.

Mutual fund investments, on the other hand, report both interest and dividend income and capital gains and losses annually. You are, therefore, always "current" on your taxes. With individual stocks and bonds you must keep an investing history of what you paid for each investment so that you'll know the capital gain or loss upon sale or maturity.

Tax Benefits of Treasury and Municipal Debt

US government ("Treasury") debt securities pay interest that is exempt from state and local income taxes. In a high-tax state such as New York, you will not need to pay the 8% state income tax on Treasury investment income as you would for, say, interest on a corporate bond. Similarly, interest income for debt of states and local governments ("municipal debt") is exempt from federal taxation. Since federal tax rates are much higher than those of any state, this municipal debt exemption is quite valuable. Unfortunately, everybody understands the tax advantage. Consequently, the typical municipal bond pays interest that is much less than it would be absent the special tax exemption. (Some municipal bonds are explicitly "taxable". These do pay normal bond yields.) Thus, you lose on the coupon most or all of what you gain from the tax treatment.

Investors in tax-exempt municipal bonds explicitly seek the

special tax treatment. In fact, no investor would buy such a bond if he/she could not realize the tax benefit. For example, an investor who does not pay New York state taxes would certainly not buy a New York tax-exempt municipal bond. As a consequence, liquidity of municipal bonds is generally poor since only a limited pool of tax-advantaged investors exists for each bond.

Keep Your Eye on the Ball !

The purpose of investing is to have fun and build wealth over time. More specifically, you want to build after-tax wealth. Thus, it seems reasonable to consider tax consequences in your investing. But there's a tendency to take this thought too far. That is, the goal is to grow after-tax wealth and not simply to minimize your taxes.

In many sports, a cardinal rule is to keep your eye on the ball. When you focus on tax reduction, you're taking your eye off the ball. Investments in which a key advantage is favorable tax treatment are most likely unsuitable for other reasons. Municipal bonds, for example, are illiquid. Virtually all partnerships are illiquid also and have poor price transparency. For those of us who prepare our own tax returns, such tax-advantaged investments become nightmares, or at least headaches, for tax reporting.

Find the investments for your portfolio that have the

"acceptable characteristics" of chapter 6 and that fit your risk tolerance. Then let the taxes fall where they may. Other people will play games to reduce their taxes while you're doing something more enjoyable.

Tax Treatments to Consider

Interest in bonds have tax liability as if they were "ordinary income"

Capital gains and dividends have preferred tax treatment

The tax system currently encourages long-term ownership (with lower taxes on gains)

US government (treasury) bonds are exempt from state and local taxes; and municipal bonds are exempt from federal taxes

Tax code limits net capital losses in any tax year to $3,000 (you can carry the excess into future tax years)

Focus on investments rather than taxes

SUMMARY GAME PLAN

The proper game plan for managing your finances is simple and straightforward. Keep expenses less than income. Pay all or most of your excess income every month to a brokerage account. Invest this accumulated cash in a manner consistent both with your personal risk tolerance and the principles of chapter 6.

Perhaps creating the brokerage account and choosing investments appear to be the more challenging steps. But these are not complicated. It's highly likely the bank you use for a checking account will offer investment/brokerage services. Just walk into your bank's local branch and ask. Further, there are many other well known firms that offer excellent service. Call one of these firms, fill out the application, and send a check for an initial deposit – perhaps just $1,000, for example. Your money will likely go straight into a money market fund. You can then choose your investments over time as you send more money to the account every month.

Truly the hardest step for almost everybody is "keep expenses less than income". As we discussed at length, be ruthless if necessary. If your "natural spending" routinely exceeds your income, then make a list of all the money you spend in a month to identify what is going wrong and where you will cut costs. This self-scrutiny may well be more psychological than it is financial. Whether by increasing income or reducing expenses, be sure to generate a consistent surplus.

Focus on living below your means, sending funds to the investment account, and choosing comfortable investments. Over time your wealth will build to the "rich level" of ten times your annual income and you will attain freedom and security for yourself and your family.

EXIT
Financial
Freedom
This Exit

APPENDIX: HEDGE FUNDS IN MORE DEPTH

Business Model is Straightforward

The business model of the hedge fund (HF) is straightforward. The HF solicits investor clients who place funds with the HF for investment. The return on invested funds pays both fees to the HF and a return to the client. Clients, not surprisingly, desire high post-fee investment returns with low volatility and low correlation to other investments.

Investors have many options to deploy their capital beginning with purchases of individual debt and equity securities to build custom portfolios. Individuals, insurance companies, not-for-profit endowments, corporate treasuries – among others – create their own portfolios. A popular alternative and complement is to purchase shares of mutual funds in which management companies earn fees to invest the investors' aggregate share proceeds. The typical mutual fund restricts itself to specific investments such as U.S. high-yield bonds or emerging market equities in order to appeal to clients with interests in these sectors. Such specialization also permits the mutual fund manager to advertise itself as expert in a narrow field rather than to make the less credible claim of "expertise in everything".

Mutual funds must operate within the constraints of the Investment Company Act of 1940 ("'40 Act") which include limits on leverage and short selling. Hedge funds and mutual funds share a similar business model with the distinction being the former's exemption from the '40 Act. Unlike mutual funds, hedge funds have great freedom to employ leverage, enter into financial contracts ("derivatives"), borrow and sell assets ("go short") and have minimal disclosure requirements. But HFs are severely restricted with respect to promoting and advertising their funds and must take money only from wealthy clients.

What the Hedge Fund Tells its Clients

Typical mutual fund activities are uncomplicated. If the fund's objective is to own corporate bonds, then it buys and holds corporate bonds with relatively little trading of such bonds. It is, for the most part, a long-only, buy-and-hold strategy. The HF's pitch to investors is quite the opposite. Hedge funds purport to be experts in finding profitable market opportunities in complex niches of the financial markets.

Hedge fund strategies tend to require high trading frequency or the establishment of partially offsetting positions or both. Hedge funds manage positions actively and embrace esoteric and ephemeral concepts.

In its marketing and its execution, HF management is expensive. That is, relative to mutual funds, hedge funds impose high fees and spend lavishly on its people and information systems. Typical funds charge a management fee of 2% of assets under management (AUM) and an incentive fee of 20% of the investors' returns. For example, if a hedge fund manager holds $1 billion of AUM and the past year's performance of this $1 billion is a 15% gain, then the manager earns $20 million (2% of $1 billion) in management fee plus another $30 million (20% of the 15% investment return on the $1 billion) incentive fee. Mutual fund fees, on the other hand, vary with the type of fund but it's not uncommon for such fees to be less than 1% of AUM.

Rationally, there's no reason for the HF investor to balk at the high fees if the net return to the investor is strong and superior to investment alternatives. If the HF fees truly buy good performance, investors will remain with the fund. A hedge fund with a good recent track record will likely keep current investors and gain new investment through its marketing of the track record. Conversely, money can quickly flee a fund with mediocre results. It's a volatile business.

Hedge Funds versus Market Efficiency

There's a remarkable clash of worldviews between bold HF marketing claims and the doctrine of "market efficiency". As a short and incomplete description, if markets are efficient, then no investor can reliably and legally outperform the market.[1] There are many caveats and qualifiers to add to that statement, but they don't invalidate the basic idea that there does not exist a "financial genius" who can, for example, reliably predict whether *IBM* common stock will outperform *McDonald's* common stock over the next year. Such a simple question – and yet there is nobody alive who would get that answer right with a probability greater than 50% (according to those who subscribe to the efficient market theory).

Both explicitly and implicitly, hedge fund marketers dispute market efficiency with the claim that the fund's traders and managers do find and exploit inefficiencies. Hedge funds may disclose their trade strategies in broad terms. The next section gives examples. But funds are loath to disclose more specific trade information to investors for fear that the alleged inefficiency will disappear when such information becomes widely known. This furtiveness heightens the allure of the hedge fund. The underlying message is often "we have secret ways to make money".

---

[1] See B. Malkiel, "A Random Walk Down Wall Street", W. W. Norton & Company, Inc., 2012.

There are financial professionals who believe "market efficiency" is, generally, a correct concept and is the right paradigm for understanding market movements. In fact, virtually all derivative pricing models invoke market efficiency. But there are also financial professionals who would label market efficiency as "wrong". This schism is so basic to the financial world that it's surprising the point is rarely debated openly. All the serious historical studies favor the efficient market view. If one could show that actual returns (*i.e.*, net of fees) to investors from hedge funds unambiguously exceeded the market benchmarks, this result would be a refutation of market efficiency.[2] Such a study does not exist to our knowledge.

Whether one subscribes to a strong, weak, or negative view of market efficiency, it is valuable to bear this efficiency question in mind while analyzing hedge funds. Given the large HF fees, why should investors believe their returns will be strong? Should hedge funds even exist? Specific funds may indeed have convincing answers to this question. Ultimately, hedge funds do add value to the economy for reasons that

---

[2] Admittedly, this could be a challenging exercise. One would need to account for leverage of the HF, the mix of assets, and eliminate the natural survivor bias. An odd element of the financial world is the lack of interest in statistical validation of portfolio management. The pharmaceutical world has its "double-blind drug trials" while money managers never get tested so rigorously.

neither the funds themselves nor the investors likely contemplate.

Examples of Hedge Fund Strategies

Hedge funds base their investment positions on a finite number of trade ideas – also called "strategies". A typical fund may have roughly ten such strategies although market conditions may not be favorable for all ideas at any specific time.

Consider first the convertible bond strategies. Convertibles are bonds that give the holder the right to trade the bond back to the issuer for a fixed number of shares of the bond issuer's equity. Hence, we say such bonds have embedded equity call options. While the equity call option makes the convertible bond more expensive than the identical bond would be without the option, the hedge fund may believe that the market gives too little value to the option. If so, the HF trader buys the convertible bond and then separately sells the equivalent equity call option. Thus, the HF is long the option within the bond but short the option from the separate option sale so that the net result is ownership of the bond issuer's default risk with no equity conversion feature. Total yield to the HF is the bond coupon plus the premium of the call option it sold. This yield will be greater than the yield of the same issuer's comparable non-convertible bond – otherwise the HF would not have executed the trade. The HF may elect to keep the bond default risk or it may hedge this risk by buying credit default swap (CDS) protection or by shorting a comparable bond, if possible.

Another example strategy is the convergence trade with U.S. Treasury securities. The most recently issued 30-year Treasury bond is the "on-the-run" long bond. Imagine a prior 30-year bond issue took place a year ago so that the outstanding bonds of that issue now have remaining maturity of 29 years. This latter is an "off-the-run" Treasury bond. It's not uncommon for the off-the-run bond to have a higher yield than the on-the-run bond. Yet it stands to reason that the yields of the two bonds should converge at some point given the near equivalence of the bonds. If the yield difference is large enough, the HF will buy the off-the-run bond and short the on-the-run bond and wait for "convergence" when its long position (off-the-run bond) will appreciate relative to its short position (on-the-run bond).

A third strategy example is the "negative basis trade". If the hedge fund can buy a corporate or sovereign bond in the market that pays a yield above LIBOR higher than the premium of the corresponding CDS, it will buy the bond and simultaneously buy CDS protection. As with the Treasury convergence trade, one expects that the bond yield spread to LIBOR should come into line with the CDS premium at which point the HF can sell both the bond and CDS position at a profit. Further, the CDS is a good hedge against the default of the bond while the HF holds this strategy.

Capital structure arbitrage is a pretentious name for a fourth strategy in which the HF takes a view that the debt of a corporate entity is valued too highly or cheaply relative to the equity of the same issuer. There exists a "Merton model" doctrine in the financial world that seeks to understand debt value in terms of equity value and volatility. Hence, a hedge fund trader may have a mathematical model that claims that market prices of the equity and debt are not consistent. If this is the case, the trader would buy the under-valued security and short the other. This is also a type of "relative value" trade. The most publicized application of this strategy in recent years pertained to collateralized debt obligations (CDOs). A few HF players bought CDO equity and shorted debt within the same CDO structure.

As a fifth and final hedge fund strategy example, consider the straightforward purchase of distressed securities. Through proprietary modeling and analysis, the HF may believe that the market has over-sold certain bonds such as sub-prime RMBS. The only method to profit from this view may be to buy these bonds with the intent to hold them for a year or longer. It is almost always the case that distressed debt is illiquid. This illiquidity necessitates the long holding period.

These limited examples demonstrate that hedge funds will take both "directional risk" and "hedged risk". The HF takes directional risks such as buying and holding distressed debt or buying gold or shorting a specific currency when it expresses deliberate views on the current market. Sophisticated hedge funds create methods to determine optimal allocation of capital across strategies that consider volatility of individual positions and correlations across positions.

Hedge Fund Financial Risks

All financial investments carry risk. We state the most obvious risk first – when a hedge fund takes a directional position such as "long gold", it will take losses if the gold value falls. Many funds worldwide have put on the long gold trade since 2008 due to various financial crises and the reactions and statements of central banks that control money supply. The market price of gold climbed markedly from 2008 to 2012, but bear in mind that the prevailing gold price represents the market's current expectations of future monetary weakness rather than simply the market's assessment of the current economic distress. Stated differently, the efficient market viewpoint is roughly that gold is just as likely to decline in value over the next year as it is to appreciate.[3]

---

[3] We should add that many investors, including hedge funds, go long gold as a hedge to the remainder of their portfolios. They reason that a fall in the value of their gold position in the future should mean that economic conditions are relatively benign such that their equities and bonds will perform reasonably. The purchase of gold is insurance against a "monetary crash" scenario

A second risk is simply that a hedge fund's models or assumptions upon which it relied to conceive trade ideas prove to be unreliable. Consider the capital structure arbitrage. The concept is highly dependent on mathematical modeling with computer programming employing plausible, but fallible, links between a firm's balance sheet and the relative value of equity and debt. Stated more plainly, trades often don't work in practice as they're drawn up in theory.

A third risk and a key weakness of the hedge fund model is leverage. Most HF strategies have low risk and provide low returns relative to the notional or par amount of the trades. A good example of this characteristic is the negative basis trade in which the HF buys a bond and then buys CDS protection. When the opportunity exists, the typical return for this pair of trades is LIBOR plus 0.2% - 0.4% per annum of the par amount. Since this return is well below the HF's target, the hedge fund will borrow as much as possible (*i.e.*, use leverage) to purchase the bond rather than use investor funds. Leverage amplifies both gains and losses. The risk of leverage to the hedge fund is not simply that losses are magnified. Rather, the HF depends for this type of borrowing on its prime broker or, potentially, another counterparty. The commitment of the prime broker to lend is short-term in nature. This lender generally has the right to terminate the transaction with one

---

if and when countries like the US and Eurozone members begin paying their debts simply by printing more currency.

day's notice or to change the haircut (loan amount) or the lending rate.

Still with the example of the negative basis trade, the HF would pledge as collateral the bond it purchased in a loan from the prime broker. The loan amount might be 80% of the bond value which means the HF uses 20% equity (investor funds) and 80% debt for the long bond position. In the CDS, it's likely the prime broker would be the counterparty and would require the HF to post margin collateral to ensure the HF's performance in this derivative transaction. This collateral pledge amount is also variable over time. The hedge fund's risk, then, is that the prime broker and other lenders will suddenly call the loans and force the HF to liquidate its positions at a loss.[4]

A fourth risk is that the client investors will pull *their* funds. The industry tends to think of hedge fund investors as providing equity. Unlike a primary equity investment in a real company – such as IBM – the HF investors expect to get their money back upon request. As with loans that are called, large-scale net outflow of investor funds causes de-leveraging (liquidation of trades) and downward pressure on HF returns. Falling returns may well lead to further investor redemptions.

[4] If lenders do cut off funding in this manner, it will likely happen at a bad time. Either the individual hedge fund's credit risk is perceived to be high or the larger market is in panic and the prime broker is trying to save itself. In either case, the HF is unlikely to be able to find another lender on short notice.

To mitigate this risk, hedge funds do place as many restrictions as is commercially possible on investor redemptions, but the threat remains.

Yet another risk is counterparty credit risk in derivative transactions and with account banks such as the prime broker. The two parties to a derivative trade generally execute a "credit support agreement" (CSA) which stipulates the terms of collateral pledging based on the evolving value of the underlying transaction. Hedge funds are typically seen as weak in their credit quality. Thus, it's not uncommon for these funds to pledge collateral to the counterparties without a reciprocal pledging of collateral from counterparties to the hedge funds ("one-way CSA"). The best risk mitigant is for the HFs to negotiate two-way collateral pledging in their CSAs if commercially possible. A more evident counterparty risk of a hedge fund is to the prime broker. This broker holds cash and securities for the HF and may at times commingle funds among different clients and with its own accounts.

Hedge funds are targets of political attack. In times of economic turmoil, there is a long tradition of public figures showering blame on financial professionals. Of course, there are times when such accusations may have a basis in truth. But there are many more occasions in which the public does not understand rising oil prices or sovereign default speculation or rising inflation and blame will fall on whomever appears to be lurking in the vicinity and not under duress.[5]

A good, current (early 2012) example of this HF risk is the attempt of Eurozone politicians to engineer a default of Greek sovereign debt without triggering CDS contracts. Various public officials believe hedge funds and other speculators are partially (or fully?) to blame for the wide debt yields of several European countries. The theory of blame states that hedge funds have been shorting government bonds, buying CDS protection, and making negative statements about sovereign creditworthiness. While all three points may be valid, it does not mean that hedge funds and speculators caused the underlying problems (though we realize this is a worthwhile discussion outside the realm of this document).

The hedge funds are simply making a "crowded", directional trade that is not all that different from many hedge funds being long gold. Or, it may well be that some funds have used a short CDS position in Greek sovereign debt as an offset to a different, but long, risk in Greece. Public officials have the goal of hurting financially whatever entities have short CDS positions on Greek debt. The lesson is that hedge funds must keep "political risk" as a consideration in their strategies.

---

[5] H. L. Mencken once said "Every complex problem has a simple, easy-to-understand, wrong answer."

Hedge Fund Legal and Ethical Risks

The hedge fund investor also bears legal and ethical risks to the behavior of the HF manager. We noted earlier the tension between the efficient market theory (EMT) and the HF business model. Hedge fund marketers will tell current and prospective investors that their firm has trade ideas that, contrary to the EMT, will routinely and significantly outperform the market. If the EMT is substantially correct for instruments the HF trades, then how would a marketer convince investors of the wisdom of investing in the hedge fund?

One strong argument would be to show investors the fund's track record of impressive returns over the past few years.[6] Good results speak for themselves. The risk, though, is that the stated results may be false, fraudulent, presented deceptively, or otherwise unreliable. Why should investors believe that the HF's stated current or historical returns are accurate? There have been hundreds of Ponzi schemes and similar frauds over

---

[6] To be more accurate in a statistical sense, this argument is not as strong as it seems. Due to "survivor bias", any hedge fund that can show a 5-year track record will, by definition, be better than the average hedge fund since many funds don't survive for 5 years. See, for example, G. N. Gregoriou, "Hedge fund survival lifetimes", *J. Asset Management*, **3**, 237-52, 2002. If HF returns are random – a simplified interpretation of EMT – then the past returns of 5-year survivors do not imply similar future returns.

the lifetime of the hedge fund industry.[7] The investor's best defenses against potential fraud of this type are numerous due diligence steps including direct meetings with the HF's auditor.

A lesser form of false reporting that an auditor may not catch stems from monthly valuation of the HF's positions. For relatively illiquid assets and derivatives, the marks (values) the HF declares may be deliberately biased. Operationally there is often a third-party firm that confirms the HF values, but this supposedly independent review may be cursory. Investors don't have the necessary information to fully vet the HF manager's valuations. The best practice for investors is to (i) review the HF's stated valuation policy and procedure, (ii) ask the HF to disclose the asset types and amounts that require indirect valuation (subjective models, for example), and (iii) speak to the auditor regarding its review and conclusions for valuation.

If traders or other staff of a hedge fund commit crimes such as insider trading, investors may suffer direct losses due to disgorgement of profits and indirect losses from mass redemption and liquidation of positions. Hedge fund strategies, unfortunately, can approach the boundary of insider trading. Consider "merger arbitrage" in which two companies announce a proposed merger at a designated target price. Some hedge funds will buy or short securities in an attempt to profit from the

---

[7] See a partial list at http://en.wikipedia.org/wiki/List_of_Ponzi_schemes .

ultimate outcome (that the deal will either close at the target price, close at a different price, or not close at all). A fund participating in this strategy believes it has an "information advantage" due to connections with bankers and industry lawyers. Even with good intentions, in this strategy there is always the possibility that the hedge fund's information becomes tainted with some "inside information".[8] Of course, a trader's intentions are not always good.

Positive Consequences of Hedge Funds

In a free society, investors should have the option to invest in private investment vehicles such as hedge funds. It may well be that the ultimate "right answer" is that the EMT consigns hedge funds to the category of sub-optimal investments. Nonetheless, investors have the right to this choice. In fact, even with this view of the world, hedge funds have a critically important role to play.

First, hedge funds are speculators and it is market speculation that creates market efficiency. The reason, for example, that there is "no arbitrage" in the relationship between

[8] One finds an interesting example in the recent book "Boomerang" (M. Lewis, W. W. Norton & Company, 2011). A large hedge fund hired a well-known academic to consult on the creditworthiness of European sovereigns. The HF provided economic and market data and asked the consultant to provide analysis and conclusions. If this academic had previously consulted for one of these governments, would later public or regulator scrutiny consider this behavior to be unethical or illegal?

a foreign currency value, its forward value, and the yield curves of the domestic and foreign currency is that market speculators watch this relationship constantly. Speculators "correct" small deviations by executing appropriate trades. Efficient markets need speculators.

Second, much of current market speculation comes from the proprietary trading desks ("prop desks") of banks. One can argue that the worldwide banking system would benefit from the transfer of these prop desks to hedge funds. As part of an established bank, the taxpayers ultimately support and backstop the prop desks even when there is statutory language to the contrary. Removing risk from the taxpayer and placing it with willing hedge fund investors while preserving the critical role of speculation benefits everybody.

As an example of the positive consequence of speculation for the market, consider an investor pondering the purchase of IBM stock. One of the best features of equity investment in a company such as IBM is the liquidity. What is the source of the liquidity? IBM, as issuer of its equity, has no obligation ever to repurchase its stock. IBM may elect to pay a dividend, but there is no guarantee it will continue to pay the dividend. If the investor did not have very high confidence that he/she would be able to sell IBM stock in the secondary market at some later time, then this would be a *terrible* investment. Think about that – why make an investment when there is no obligation for repayment and any future payment is discretionary? With no secondary market, there is not even a good estimate of the stock's value. Philosophically, one could say there is "no value" if there is no buyer regardless of the underlying fundamentals.

Thus, the existence of liquidity in a secondary market in which other players will bid for the investor's IBM stock is of tremendous value both to the investor and to IBM. Yet IBM does not create this secondary market and has little influence over its existence. Further, the government does not create or facilitate this market, either. Secondary markets are the spontaneous and highly fortuitous creation of the human beings attracted to capital raising and the capital markets. Call them speculators or gamblers or middle-men. By any name, capitalism would be stillborn without them.

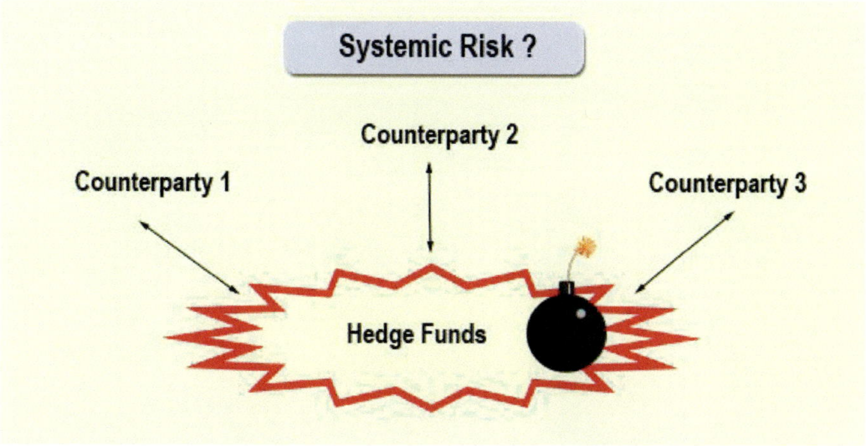

Some politicians and financial regulators believe hedge funds contribute to "systemic risk" through their trading in derivatives. As the figure above depicts, the concern is that a hedge fund will "blow up" (default on its obligations) and cause sufficient losses to induce one or more of its derivative counterparties to "blow up" as well. We believe this risk is over-stated. Collateral agreements protect the counterparties from derivative losses. In addition, no counterparty would permit its exposure to a particular hedge fund to be so great that the hedge fund's failure would bring down the counterparty.

GLOSSARY

Acceptable Investments

Investments that you understand, are consistent with your risk tolerance, and have good liquidity and price transparency

Adjustable-Rate Mortgage (ARM)

Mortgage loan in which the interest rate the borrower pays changes (or "adjusts") over time due to a contractual link to a specified interest rate index

Arbitrage

Term that has somewhat different meanings in different context with the most prevalent definition being "a transaction in which the investor earns positive return with zero risk"

Bankruptcy

A legal proceeding involving a person or business as debtor that is unable to make payment obligations to one or more creditors

Barter

The act of trading goods and services between two or more parties without the use of money

Beat the Market

When an investor, portfolio manager, fund or other investment specialist produces a better return than a comparable market benchmark

Bid Price

The price a dealer is willing to pay you for an asset you wish to sell. The bid price is less than the offer price.

Bid-Offer Spread

The difference between a dealer's offer price and bid price for the same asset. This difference is effectively the fee the dealer earns for acting as market intermediary between buyers and sellers.

Board of Directors

A group of individuals that are elected to act as representatives of the stockholders of a public corporation to supervise company management and to make decisions on major company issues

Bond

A financial instrument that represents a long from the investor / creditor to the bond issuer / debtor. The bond documents specify the maturity (bond repayment period) and interest payments

Bond yield

The percentage return that the investor will receive if he/she buys the bond at current market price and if the bond makes all future principal and interest payments

Book value

For an asset, the value at which the asset is carried on a balance sheet; for a company, the book value of assets minus the liabilities at par

Broker

An individual or a firm that charges a fee or commission and acts as intermediary for buy and sell orders submitted by an investor

Brokerage account

An investment account with a licensed brokerage firm in which the investor deposits funds and places investment orders through the brokerage – the account and all cash and assets are the property of the investor

Call Option

A formal and documented financial contract that gives an investor the right (but not the obligation) to buy a stock, bond, commodity, or other instrument at a specified price within a specified time period

Capital gain

A profit from the sale of an investment or property

Capital loss

A loss from the sale of an investment or property

CD (certificate of deposit)

A savings certificate entitling the bearer to receive interest and return of the original investment generally with fixed maturity date and interest rate, repayment guaranteed by the FDIC for bank issuers and the NCUA (National Credit Union Administration) for credit union issuers

Checking account

An account with a bank in which a customer deposits cash and pays bills to others by writing checks drawn against the account

Commodity

Any good exchanged in commerce including agricultural products, energy products, and metals

Common stock

A security that represents ownership in a corporation; common stockholders are at the bottom of the priority ladder for ownership structure-in the event of liquidation, common shareholders have rights to a company's assets only after bondholders, preferred shareholders and other debt holders and creditors have been paid in full

Convertible preferred stock

Preferred stock that includes an option for the holder to convert the preferred shares into a specified number of shares of common stock, usually any time after a predetermined date

Corporate bonds

Debt securities issued by corporations - they are generally considered higher risk than government bonds

Coupon

The annualized interest rate stated on a bond at issuance; the frequency of coupon payments and the details of computing the dollar amount of such payments will vary from one bond to another

Credit rating

An assessment of the creditworthiness of individuals, corporations, municipalities, or countries generally provided by well established, nationally known rating providers

Credit Score

A numerical value in the range 300 – 850 provided independently by several distinct companies that purports to show relative likelihood of debt repayment by adult consumers. For example, Jane Smith's credit score of 750 implies she is more like to pay a mortgage, or auto loan, or credit card than Bob Jones with a credit score of 500.

Debt

An amount of money borrowed by one party ("borrower") from another ("lender") in which the borrower has a legal obligation to repay the lender

Debt-to-Income (DTI)

In a mortgage loan, the ratio of the borrower's total monthly debt payments to this borrower's total monthly gross income

Default

The failure to promptly pay the contractual interest or principal of a bond or other debt instrument when due

Discount Broker

Stockbroker who executes buy and sell orders at a rate of commission lower than those charged by full-service brokers, and usually gives little to no investment advice

Diversification

A risk management technique that mixes a variety of investments within a portfolio so that the loss of value of any one position will not be overly punitive

Dividend

Payment to common equity or preferred equity investors from after-tax earnings or borrowed money at the discretion of the Board of Directors

Efficient market

Market where all pertinent information is available to all participants at the same time, and where prices respond immediately to such information, stock markets are generally the best example of efficient markets

Face value

The value written on a banknote, share certificate, or coin, in the case of a bond it is the payment to be made by the borrower at maturity

FDIC (Federal Deposit Insurance Corporation)

The U.S. government entity insuring deposits in the U.S. against bank failure. The FDIC will insure deposits up to $250,000 per account with banks that are member firms

Financial advisor

A person or organization employed by an individual or mutual fund to manage assets or provide investment advice

Financial Asset

A resource with economic value that an individual, corporation, country, or other entity owns or controls with the expectation that it will provide future financial benefit

Fixed-Rate Mortgage (FRM)

Mortgage loan in which the interest rate the borrower pays remains at the same percentage of outstanding principal over time

Foreclosure

Action by a mortgage lender to enforce its right to seize real estate from the borrower due to the borrower's failure for a prolonged period of time to make loan payments

Free market

A market economy based on supply and demand with relatively little governmental control, also a philosophy that willing buyers and willing sellers should be free to transact and that such transactions are beneficial to both buyer and seller

Full-service broker

A stockbroker who provides a portfolio of investment services, such as financial advice, market research, stock recommendations, and order execution

Futures contract

A contractual agreement, generally made on the trading floor of a futures exchange, to buy or sell a particular commodity or financial investment at a pre-determined price in the future, a key feature of such contracts is that both buyer and seller must post collateral to guarantee that each will honor the future obligation

Gambling

Games of chance, or wagers on events of uncertain outcomes with arguably no economic or societal benefit

Government bonds

Debt securities issued by a sovereign government to support government spending and backed by the full faith and credit of the government. Government bonds in the United States include the "savings bond", Treasury bonds, notes, and bills, and Treasury inflation-protected securities (TIPS)

Hedge

Making an investment to reduce the risk of adverse price movements in an asset or portfolio, normally a hedge consists of taking an offsetting position in a related security

Hedge fund

An aggressively managed portfolio of investments that uses significant leverage and a mixture of long, short, and derivative positions with the goal of generating high returns that are uncorrelated with the overall market

Hostile takeover

A takeover by an outside firm or individual that is not supported by the target company's Board of Directors, shareholders may approve such a takeover bid regardless of the advice of the Board

Index fund

A type of mutual fund with a portfolio constructed to match or track the components of a market index, such as the Standard & Poor's 500 Index (S&P 500), an index fund is said to provide broad market exposure, low operating expenses and low portfolio turnover

Inflation

The rate at which the general level of prices for goods and services is rising, and, subsequently, purchasing power of the currency is falling

Insider trading

The buying or selling of a security by someone who has access to material, nonpublic information about the security, an example of legal insider trading is the sale of stock by a company executive within an SEC-approved timeframe and with public notice of the transaction, many other forms of insider trading are prohibited by securities laws

Interest

The negotiated fee that a borrower will pay a lender, typically expressed as an annual percentage rate and paid on frequent, pre-determined payment dates up to the loan maturity

Investment-grade

A bond with a credit rating from a credit rating agency that is BBB- (or its equivalent rating) or better

Investment portfolio

A compilation of assets working in concert designed to achieve a specific investment objective based on parameters such as risk tolerance, return target, time horizon, asset preference, and liquidity needs

IPO (Initial Public Offering)

The first sale of stock by a private company to the public, dangerous for investors since there is no efficient market in the stock prior to this first sale, hence the post-IPO stock price may rise or fall dramatically

Junk bond

High-yield or non-investment-grade bond, a bond with a credit rating from a credit rating agency that is BB+ (or its equivalent rating) or worse, such bonds have higher default risk relative to investment-grade bonds but, despite the pejorative name, are reasonable investments under conditions of proper risk tolerance and diversification

Leverage

Use of borrowed money in one form or another to make an investment, returns are magnified (both positive and negative) with leverage

Liability

A company's legal debts or obligations that arise during the normal course of business operations

Lien

Gives the lien holder the right to seize property against which the lien is established in order to force repayment of a debt or other contractual obligation

Liquid

An asset that is easily converted into cash with minimal impact to the price received

Loan maturity

Date when the final loan principal amount becomes due and payable

Loan-to-Value (LTV)

In a mortgage loan, the ratio of the outstanding loan amount to the value of the real estate pledged as collateral for the loan

Market loss

If and when the current market value of an investment falls below the value at which the investor purchased the investment, he/she has suffered a market loss

Market value

The current quoted price at which investors buy or sell an asset at a given time

Maturity date

The date on which the principal amount of a note, draft, acceptance bond or other debt instrument becomes due, similar to "Loan maturity"

Mortgage

A form of borrowing in which the borrower pledges real estate as collateral for the loan

Mortgage-backed securities (MBS)

A type of asset-backed security that is secured by a mortgage or collection of mortgages, buyers of MBS become the lenders for the mortgages

Municipal bonds

Debt securities issued by sub-sovereign governments such as states, municipalities, cities, counties, et cetera, to finance spending. Such bonds are often exempt from federal taxation and from most state and local taxes for investors residing in the state or local region of the bond issuer

Mutual fund

A regulated investment fund that pools the contributions of many small investors and hires a financial firm to invest and manage the shared portfolio

Nasdaq/NASDAQ

A computerized system that facilitates trading and provides price quotations on more than 5,000 of the more actively traded over-the-counter stocks, the world's first electronic stock market, when founded in 1971 the original acronym was "National Association of Securities Dealers Automated Quotations"

Offer Price

Also known as the "Ask Price" – it is the price a dealer is willing to receive from you for an asset you wish to buy. The offer price is greater than the bid price.

Options

A financial contract sold by one party to another party that gives the buyer the right, but not the obligation, to buy or sell a security or other financial asset or commodity at an agreed-upon price during a certain period of time or on a specific date

Par

Essentially the face value of a bond or other security from which an interest payment is computed, when a par value is quoted for common stock, there is little practical meaning

Partnership

A business organization in which two or more individuals manage and operate the business, both owners are equally and personally liable for the debts from the business (if the partnership is not incorporated in a manner that limits liability)

Ponzi scheme

A form of fraud in which belief in the success of a nonexistent enterprise or investment strategy is fostered by the payment of quick returns to the first investors from money invested by later investors, such schemes must always grow in order to sustain payments and they will always collapse

Preferred stock

A class of investment in a corporation that has a higher claim on the assets and earnings than common stock but, unlike common stock, does not convey ownership of the corporation

Price transparency

The accessibility of information on recent transactions the current order flow for a particular stock, allowing knowledge of the bids and offers at the various price levels

Principal

The amount invested as opposed to the dividends or interest paid on this invested amount

Put option

A formal and documented financial contract that gives an investor the right (but not the obligation) to sell a stock, bond, commodity, or other instrument at a specified price within a specified time period

Refinance

Borrowing from a new lender in order to pay the debt owed to an existing lender

Risk

The probability that an investment's actual return will differ from the expected (or average) return, risk includes the possibility of both gain and loss relative to the expected return

Risk tolerance

The degree of variability in investment returns that an individual is willing to withstand

Risk-free

An investment for which there is essentially no probability of receiving a return above or below the expected return, always associated with a specific tenor ("time horizon"), an example is a 1-month Treasury bill for a time horizon of 1 month

Savings account

A deposit account held at a bank or other financial institution that provides principal security and a modest interest rate

Securities Investor Protection Corporation (SIPC)

A nonprofit corporation created by an act of Congress in 1970 to protect the clients of brokerage firms that are forced into bankruptcy, provides brokerage customers up to $500,000 coverage for cash and securities missing from the bankrupt firm with a limit of $250,000 for cash

Short selling

The selling of a security that a seller does not actually own, rather, the seller borrows the security from another investor in order to deliver it to the buyer, the short seller will ultimately need to buy the security in order to convey it back to the security lender, the short seller will profit if the price at which he/she later buys the security is less than the price at which he/she sold (short) the security

Speculative grade bond

See "Junk bond"

Stock

A type of security that signifies ownership in a corporation and represents a claim on part of the corporation's assets and earnings – see "Common Stock"

Systemic risk

The unlikely but devastating possibility that numerous financial firms, governments, and central banks may fail within a common timeframe

Tax liability

The total amount of tax that an entity is legally obligated to pay to an authority as the result of the occurrence of a taxable event

Treasury bill

A short-term debt obligation backed by the U.S. government with a maturity of one year or less, these "T-bills" pay no interest, thus the investor pays a purchase price that is a small amount (the "discount") less than the face value in order to receive an effective interest return

Treasury debt securities

Any borrowing of the U.S. government in the form of securities issued to the public, includes Treasury bonds, notes, and bills, see also "Government bonds"

Trustee

A person or firm that holds or administers property or assets or legal rights for the benefit of a third party, for example, corporate bond offerings have Trustees that monitor the payment of interest and principal to the investors as well as other legal obligations of the borrower, if the borrower violates any obligation, the Trustee will act on behalf of investors to enforce their legal rights

About the Authors

From one of the authors' twenty years of financial experience with Wall Street firms and investments, we distill the habits and rules that build wealth. The ideas are simple and work for everybody. Put these principles in action today to create freedom and security for yourself and your family. Generate the capacity to support loved ones and help others.